PORTRAIT OF
KENDAL AND THE KENT VALLEY

By the same author

PORTRAIT OF THE HOWGILLS AND THE
UPPER EDEN VALLEY

Poetry
VOICES ROUND A STAR
THE BECKWALKER
SELECTED POEMS
WESTMORLAND POEMS
SIMON'S GARDEN

Portrait of
KENDAL AND THE
KENT VALLEY

by

Michael Finch

Michael Finch.
15 . XI . '88

Photographs by
H. MARTIN GARDNER

ROBERT HALE · LONDON

ISBN 0 7090 1285 3

Robert Hale Limited
Clerkenwell House
Clerkenwell Green
London EC1R 0HT

Photoset by Rowland Phototypesetting Limited
Printed in Great Britain by
St Edmundsbury Press, Bury St Edmunds, Suffolk

Contents

Illustrations

6

Acknowledgements

Anyone writing about Kendal will inevitably owe a considerable debt to two people in particular: Cornelius Nicholson, whose *Annals of Kendal* was published in 1832; and John F. Curwen, whose *Kirkbie-Kendall* followed over half a century later, in 1900.

These books are the 'standard works', but they have been, alas, out of print for many years. Strangely I am able to claim a vicarious connection with both authors, for a few years ago I happened to make last-minute corrections to the proofs of my *Selected Poems* in the very room that had once been the architect's office of John Curwen. This was at No. 28 Highgate, one of the most attractive houses in Kendal. There also, in 1825, Cornelius Nicholson set up his printing press, and he later wrote his *Annals of Kendal* in one of the rooms destined to become the good offices of that eminent Mayor of Kendal, Titus Wilson. However, as my book is concerned not only with the town of Kendal itself, but also with the wider area which once made up the Barony of Kendal, I owe a great debt to many other people, some of whom must for ever remain anonymous. Of those I am able to acknowledge, I should like to thank R. D. Humber for permission to use information from his *Heversham*; and M. Davies-Shiel for similar permission with regard to his *Wool is my Bread*.

My thanks are also due to James Cropper, Fr Thomas Walsh, Oliver Turnbull and William Parrott for the loan of many very useful books; and to Christine Strickland, of the local history section of the Kendal Branch of the Cumbria County Library, for considerable help and advice; to Lawrence James of Sedbergh School, for the loan of much valuable material; to the Literary Executor of the late Margaret Cropper for permission to quote many lines; and to Gawith, Hoggarth and Co. Ltd and J. W. Dunderdale for much useful information.

Lastly, I should like to thank my friend Martin Gardner, for once again providing photographs that capture so excellently the mood of the area.

To Simon and Jonathan

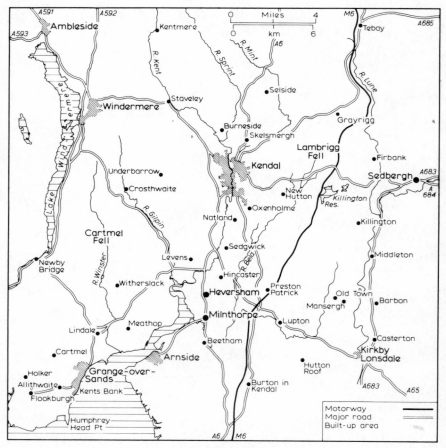

The Kent Valley

1

The Guardian at the Gate

At noon, five days before the Christmas of 1799, William and Dorothy Wordsworth walked into Kendal from the direction of Sedbergh where they had spent the night. The eleven-mile journey had taken them about three hours along a road, Wordsworth later informed his friend Coleridge, which had been 'a terrible up and down road'. For the rest of the day the brother and sister, unknown, unrecognized, anxious to buy some furniture for their new home, and order more, remained in the town. It is not known which tradesmen they visited nor at which Kendal inn they stayed, but the following morning they set off in a hired post-chaise laden with some of their purchases on their way to the small house at Town Head, Grasmere, which would for ever be associated with them and which would later be known as Dove Cottage.

In such a manner did the Wordsworths arrive in the valley they have made famous. At Kendal, a town in another valley, they grabbed their furniture and moved on. We are not going to follow them. I say this emphatically simply to explain that this is not another book about the Lake District posing as one about Kendal, even though Kendal can be truly named 'The Gateway to the Lakes'. I intend, rather, to stand at the gate and look about, to linger on the threshold, to become, for a while anyway, the 'Guardian at the Gate'. However, I must be honest and admit that without the Wordsworths and their influence it might have been difficult to have a book on Kendal published. I shall never forget the look my publisher gave me.

11

'We could hardly consider a book about Aylesbury, say, or Stratford,' he said shaking his head sadly.

At which I replied, knowing I might never dare to show my face south of the Avon again: 'Quite, but Kendal is a very different case.'

Just how different I intend now to reveal.

When speaking of Kendal one must learn to distinguish between four possible uses: for the barony, the ward, the town, and the dale. For Kendal really means Kent Dale, the dale or valley through which the River Kent flows on its relatively short course, some twenty miles only, from its source in the hills above Kentmere to its estuary which forms the north-eastern part of Morecambe Bay. Our forefathers would have had little problem as far as the town was concerned since they usually gave it the full name of Kirkby Kendale, 'the village or farmstead with a church in the Kent Valley'. What, however, of the barony and the ward?

The area, which for hundreds of years was known as the County of Westmorland, was divided by the Normans into two baronies in order to govern it more easily, but more importantly, so that it might be successfully defended against the Scots who until the Norman Conquest owned it more often than not. When the Norman surveyors came north to make their definitive record of livestock, land and ownership for what became known as Domesday Book, apart from the small township of Patton, land north of Kirkby Kendale was not included, although many nearby places a little further south like Levens, Beetham and Burton were. Kendal Castle seems at that time to have been situated near the southern limit of the Scottish kingdom, and until William Rufus took possession of Carlisle in 1092 it remained, some have claimed, north of the Border!

The two baronies were the Barony of Westmorland, often referred to as the Barony of Appleby because Appleby was its garrison, and the Barony of Kendal. The baronies were further divided into four wards, a term which reflects the unsettled nature of the Border regions and carries the meaning of keeping or protecting as in the ward of a castle or, as we still use it, of a hospital. The East and West Wards were in the Barony of Westmorland, and the Kendal and Lonsdale Wards in Kendal taking their names from the valleys of the Kent and the Lune. So we must watch our 'Kendals' closely, at least until we have 'got the knack'! In those happy phrases 'Kendal bowmen' and 'Kendal green', for instance, the Kendal part has a different meaning. The 'bowmen' would be all those throughout the whole barony whom the feudal lord could call to arms in times of trouble by right of service, while 'green' was the woollen cloth produced in the Parish of Kendal, although later the term came to mean a particular shade of green.

My book is as much 'bowmen' as 'green' in so far as it is concerned with the history and traditions of the towns, villages and hamlets situated in the old Barony of Kendal, but I admit freely that it might have been possible to devote a whole book, if not two books, to Kendal Town itself had that been my task. The area I have chosen forms the south-west part of Cumbria, which means in effect the land south of the mountains of the Lake District, although, as I have said, the River Kent has a fairly dizzy beginning. This means that some places like Grasmere, Ambleside and Windermere which were at one time within the Kendal Barony are excluded since they have received much attention elsewhere. In compensation I have included the Cartmel Peninsula, which until 1974 was part of Lancashire.

Of the two baronies in the County of Westmorland Kendal was always the smaller in area though the more densely populated, and the greater settlement of Kendal was simply a matter of geography. Appleby might be fairly well settled along the fertile Eden Valley but for the most part the countryside was harsh, uninviting fell-land, difficult to inhabit, with much of it many hundreds of feet above sea-level. In contrast Kendal, while including some high ground to the north, was for the most part gentler country creeping down gradually to sea-level with a very much more temperate climate. Often I have been amazed at the contrast in the weather conditions between my home, in Ravenstonedale, and Kendal, a distance of barely twenty miles. A dismal, rain-squalled day can burst into sun and song suddenly at a point a little beyond Grayrigg on the Kendal road, though I must admit it has been occasionally the other way round!

Something of the difference in population density resulting from the easier climate may be understood from the number of parishes and townships situated on either side of the boundary between the Kendal and West Wards. Whereas the West Ward boundary marked the southern extent of Patterdale, Shap Rural, Orton and Tebay; if regarded from the Kendal side it was the northern limit of Great and Little Langdales, Grasmere, Rydal and Loughrigg, Ambleside, Troutbeck, Kentmere, Longsleddale, Fawcett Forest, Whinfell, Patton, and Grayrigg.

It will be necessary to return to the baronies, wards and their folk later, but first it is important to take a look at the land itself, and as there is one lively feature which dominates all else, let us consider the River Kent.

The River Kent

During their occupation of Britain the Romans constructed a road from Ambleside to Brougham which crossed over the highest point, at 2,718 feet, of what are called for convenience the Kentmere Fells. This 'top', though small if compared with the greater heights visible a little to the north-west, is named after the Roman road, High Street. It is in this region in the Parish of Patterdale that the waters of the infant Kent have their gathering ground. On the southern slopes of High Street the fellside drops away suddenly leaving a craggy rock-face from which a waterfall or, as they are termed locally, a 'force', gushes at Hall Cove dropping far down to the floor of the valley. The Kent is on its way; soon to be joined by smaller streams, or 'sykes', which drain Froswick and Ill Bell on the western side of the river, and Kentmere Pike and Shipman Knotts on the east. However, between its beginning and its proceeding the Kent comes to a brief pause, for where there was always a slight natural widening of the valley a dam constructed during the nineteenth century makes the small lake of the Kentmere Reservoir. This damming of the Kent was to ensure a steady flow of water to turn the wheels of the many mills dotted along the river's banks. If we forget the reservoir and the mills for a moment and continue on downstream, we come by the small village of Kentmere to Staveley where the course turns due east suddenly, but after a short while swings back south-eastwards to receive, at Burneside, the waters of the River Sprint. Thus enforced the Kent speeds on towards Kendal taking the waters of the River Mint about half a mile north of the town. The course through Kendal is a swerving one, but once through, it loops northwards at Watercrook, but soon continues more or less southwards sweeping briefly westward at Levens for a mile or so before it loops once again into its estuary. Here it takes from the north the waters of the River Gilpin, and the River Bela from the south-east. The Bela has come by Milnthorpe which was once the only port in the County of Westmorland. From source to estuary the distance is barely twenty miles, but in that space the river has dropped over two thousand feet. I have only plotted the course of the Kent in the briefest way and it is necessary to return to Kentmere and look more closely, but not before I have said a little about the river's name.

The Westmorland River Kent and the Berkshire Kennet have the same origin, and the name almost certainly means 'from the hills' or 'from the heights'. In the case of the Kent, of course, the hills or heights are very much greater than those from which the Kennet flows. The names of rivers are very old, but often they have a simple and obvious meaning, derived from some observation of the river's characteristics. The Eden, for instance, means simply 'water'; the Lune 'full' or 'whole'. The difficulty for scholars, who seem to complicate matters with their theories, arises through lack of records, for the names were in use long before they were ever written down. The Romans, who did write things down, Latinized local names which did not help much, but as far as river names were concerned they were very late on the scene. The first records do not appear in English until the eighth century, but the English adopted the older forms, so that to learn the exact word from which the Kent and Kennet take their name would mean delving into the remote Celtic past which is impossible to do. However, I have a healthy respect for tradition unless it is obvious nonsense. In this case I believe that the name of the River Kent does mean 'from the hills'. John F. Curwen in his book *Kirkbie-Kendall* states that the name is Celtic in origin, and 'with its signification still retained in a Welsh word implying a district of rolling hills'. The hills are there all right, though Curwen is inaccurate when he says that the name was always written 'Can' until Camden's time. William Camden, I should say in passing, was headmaster of Westminster School and perhaps the first antiquary whose *Britannia* written in Latin came out in 1586.

The name appears as 'Kient' in 1205, and in the Assize Rolls for Westmorland between the years 1256 and 1329 it is written 'Kenet' or sometimes 'Keent'. However, I did discover a significant 'Can' in Michael Drayton's long topographical poem 'Polyolbion' which he completed in 1622. There Drayton speaks of the County of Westmorland:

> Where Can first creeping forth, her feet hath scarcely found,
> But gives that dale her name, where Kendal town doth stand,
> For making of our cloth scarce matched in all the land.

One of my favourite pastimes is delving into Drayton's 'Polyolbion' and I would like to treat you to more, but enough of Can, Keent and Kenet for the moment. On to Kentmere!

Kentmere

It was in 1692, towards the end of his life, that Thomas Machell, the Rector of Kirkby Thore, near Appleby, passed by Kentmere on horseback. Machell enjoyed his circuitous journeys, with notebook always at the ready in which to record observations, draw plans of buildings and make diagrams of armorial bearings he might see in the windows of churches. His keen eye has been invaluable in the study of Westmorland's history, and although he rose to be chaplain to King Charles II he remained very much a local in his interests. Machell's copious notes were recorded in six large manuscript volumes which are safely lodged in the Dean and Chapter Library in Carlisle; they were the main source for *The History and Antiquities of Westmorland and Cumberland* which Richard Burn and Joseph Nicolson brought out in 1777. When Machell came to Kentmere he was on a round-trip from Windermere.

The water of Kentmere, he noted, was some half a mile long and had a boat; it was good for two kinds of trout and in winter was a haven for as many as thirty-seven wild swans, with 'a great store of wild duck'. As to the size of the mere Machell was accurate enough; it had been described over a hundred years earlier in 1577 as 'a poole a myle compasse', and so it must have remained until it was drained some time in about 1840 to make more pasture land, a move that was to have two important repercussions.

Laverock Bridge – the River Mint at Mealbank

Firstly, it was discovered that the mere-bed contained a deposit of diatomite, the fossilized remains of microscopic, unicellular algae, which could be excavated and, in fact, still is being; and secondly that the flow of water into the river became less constant which seriously affected the operations of the many mills along the Kent Valley. This made it necessary to solve the problem by constructing the Kentmere Head Reservoir, as it was originally called, and rightly; since Kentmere should be reserved for the small hamlet with its hall and church, approached only by the one road which runs parallel with the river, unless, of course, it is approached on foot from the surrounding hills!

The draining of Kentmere, which was not entirely successful, and the mining operations, have meant that today there is a much smaller mere on the site of the earlier one. Machell mentioned a boat on the mere; what he could not have known was that there were also boats beneath the water's surface; for some years ago, in 1955, the excavation work unearthed two canoe-like boats, thought to be of the tenth century. The better of the two specimens is now in the National Maritime Museum, while fragments of the other are in the museum at Kendal. These finds give a positive clue that the region was inhabited from early times, even if there was no other evidence, but there is also the site of an ancient British settlement of the second century situated south of the hamlet, on the east side of the river. There may be seen the foundations of several hut-circles in an enclosure which takes up about three-quarters of an acre. It was small communities like this that the Romans encountered when they arrived in the area.

Machell, as I said, came to Kentmere along the road from the direction of Windermere and Ings, but in November 1799, only a few months before he was to buy his furniture in Kendal with his sister, William Wordsworth spent the night in Kentmere in the company of his brother John and Coleridge. The party had walked from Bampton, skirted the banks of Haweswater, then a small lake, and approached Kentmere from Longsleddale, that is, from the east, having seen that low cloud hiding High Street would make it impossible to reach Ambleside before nightfall. One hopes for their sakes that the Kentmere accommodation on this forced visit was of a higher standard than that described in

The Kent Valley above Kentmere

an account of a Kentmere caravansary of 1820, when the floor was 'bespread with tubs, pans, chairs, piggins, dishes, tins, and other equipage of a farmer's kitchen. In the dusk of evening, and the darkness of the house, the things were only just visible.' On that same occasion the traveller slept in a bed with curtains 'composed of patches of old paper hangings of different patterns pasted together suspended from hooks in the ceiling.' However, the bed was most likely comfortable enough, and if one remembers that a piggin was a milking-pail, with nothing mucky about it, things were not so bad in the farmhouse either. Had Dorothy Wordsworth been in the party we might have been given a glimpse of their Kentmere hostel, but she was not there on that occasion. The following day the trio crossed the Garburn Pass to Windermere, and went on to Hawkshead by ferry. It was, Wordsworth recorded, 'a rainy and raw day'.

The little church of St Cuthbert's, Kentmere, is delightfully situated at the head of the valley. It has been considerably restored with some alterations being quite recent, though the main restoration work was carried out in 1866 at about the same time that so many village churches were undergoing similar treatment. There is a tradition that there was a church at Kentmere in earlier times, possibly as early as the ninth century; for it is likely that the monks from Lindisfarne, fleeing from the Danes in the year 875 and bearing the incorrupt body of St Cuthbert together with St Oswald's head, may have rested at Kentmere for a while during their seven years of wandering. There is no certain record in Kentmere, neither is Kentmere mentioned in the list of places that are known; it is certain, for instance, that Cliburn and Dufton, near Appleby, were stopping places, and Clifton, some three miles south of Penrith; all these three are mentioned in the list compiled by Prior Wessington in 1416. But the leg of the journey from Clifton to Furness would have brought them to Kentmere had they taken the most direct route, the Roman road over High Street, which is more than likely.

The amazing act of obedience on the part of the monks, and it must be remembered that St Cuthbert had died some ninety years previously, so that they were bearing a relic and not the body of someone they had known, has captured the imaginations of many. There are several Latin verses recording their loyalty and zeal; and Sir Walter Scott brought them into 'Marmion'. We know that they traversed Northumberland, Cumberland, Westmorland, Lancashire, Durham, Yorkshire and part of Scotland; and that they tried unsuccessfully to cross over to Ireland only to be shipwrecked off the coast of Galloway. But eventually they settled, in the early part of the year 883, at Chester-le-Street where St Cuthbert's body remained for a hundred and thirteen years until it was moved to Durham, an event Scott recalled:

> And, after many wanderings past,
> He chose his lordly seat at last
> Where his cathedral, huge and vast,
> Looks down upon the Wear:
> There deep in Durham's Gothic shade
> His relics are in secret laid.

Scott is, of course, referring to the fact that it is not really known exactly where St Cuthbert's body does lie in the cathedral, but amid uncertainties is the certain fact that Kentmere Church, like Cliburn, Dufton and Clifton is dedicated to him, though Hawkshead, where at one time the relic was thought to have rested, has adopted St Michael, the archangel, about whom there is no doubt!

Inside Kentmere Church, where the nave and chancel are undivided, a common feature of many of the smaller Westmorland churches, there is a memorial tablet to Bernard Gilpin who had been born at Kentmere Hall in 1517. The bronze tablet was designed by the Keswick School of Industrial Arts in 1901, and is more modest than the great crown of thorns to his honour in Kendal Parish Church.

Bernard Gilpin

Bernard was the fourth son of Edwin Gilpin of Kentmere. Although it is uncertain where he went to school, he evidently did well enough to go up to Queen's College, Oxford, where he took his degree in 1533 and became a fellow of his college. Some seven years later he seems to have forsaken Queen's for the new college founded by Cardinal Wolsey. This was Christ's College or, as it is known today, Christ Church College, and was built

out of the proceeds of the dissolution of several of the smaller
religious houses with the full acquiescence it should be added, of
the Papacy. These were early days in the story of the Reformation! At this time Gilpin was still a firm defender of the Old
Religion and upheld orthodoxy against several reformers, including Bishop Hooper of Worcester and the Italian scholar,
Peter Martyr, who had been appointed Professor of Divinity at
Oxford.

Leaving the university at the age of thirty-five and, it was
said, badly 'shaken in faith', Gilpin became for a time priest-in-
charge of Norton, a parish in the Durham Diocese, where his
uncle, Bishop Tunstall, was in a good position to help his
promising nephew. However, Tunstall did not seem to realize to
what extent his nephew was 'bitten' by the new ideas of the
reformers until the priest of Norton resigned his living and
disappeared abroad. Gilpin returned to England in 1556 at the
height of the Marian persecutions, not a good time to return, but
the uncle, ever indulgent, appointed him Archdeacon of Durham and Rector of Easington. Soon charges of heresy were made
against him, thirteen articles in all, but the Bishop was able to
dismiss them, and Gilpin resigned the archdeaconry. Instead,
the good uncle offered him the living of Houghton-le-Spring
which carried an income of £400, a vast sum in those days.
Gilpin remained at Houghton for the rest of his life, and the
parsonage assumed, according to one eye-witness, the magni-
tude and appearance of an episcopal palace, and Gilpin's hospi-
tality was the admiration of the kingdom. At least he seems to
have learnt the ropes at Wolsey's college.

Queen Elizabeth offered Gilpin the Bishopric of Carlisle,
though his uncle, Bishop Tunstall, had refused the Elizabethan
settlement and had died under house-arrest in Lambeth Palace
after refusing to swear the Oath of Supremacy and being deprived of his diocese, in 1559. Gilpin refused preferment in the
church, and also refused the provostship of his old Oxford
college, Queen's; deciding to remain at Houghton, where he
founded a Free Grammar School in 1574, and set up almshouses
for the Poor, many of whose sons he educated at his own expense.
There were usually some twenty-three or twenty-four boys on
whom he 'bestowed meat, drink, and clothes and education'.
Many of these went on to universities, among whom was

another Kentmere lad, a member of Gilpin's own family, Henry Ayray, who went on to become Provost of Queen's. As it happened there already existed a special connection between Queen's College, Oxford, and Westmorland. This had begun in 1340 when Robert de Egglesfield founded the college as a compliment to the wife of Edward III, Queen Philippa, to whom he was confessor. Besides being chaplain to the Queen, Egglesfield happened to be Rector of Brough; hence the connection. By the terms of the original college statutes certain preference in the choice of scholars was given to the founder's family and to the natives of Westmorland and Cumberland. Many men who began their education in the small Westmorland village schools were to go on to become fellows of the college, and several, like Ayray, became provost.

Bernard Gilpin died on the 4th of March, 1583, and was buried in his own church at Houghton. Such, in brief, were the circumstances of the life of the 'Apostle of the North', a man very much of his time, not to say a time-server. It depends upon one's sympathies whether one sees Tunstall or Gilpin as the champion of the North. It was as though Gilpin himself saw all weighed in the balance, defending orthodoxy early in life, only to expound with fervour the new ideas later; but many from the Kentmere area, from Skelsmergh, and the town of Kendal itself, would have been prepared to give their lives for the religion that had served England for close on a thousand years. Gilpin was a persuasive preacher by all accounts, and perhaps he improved. Here is a sample: 'The two wells of this realm, Oxford and Cambridge: they are almost dried up,' he proclaimed in a sermon preached in the presence of King Edward VI, in 1552. 'The cruel Philistines abroad, enemies of Christ's Gospel, have stopped the springs of the faithful Abraham. The decay of students is so great, there are scarce left of every thousand an hundred – there is entering into England more blind ignorance, superstition, and infidelity, than ever was under the Romish bishops, your Realm (which I am sorry to speak) shall become more barbarous than Sythia.' In view of which, it was perhaps a mercy that the weak Edward did not live to see the day.

Kentmere Hall, for so long the home of the Gilpin family, though they were never Lords of the Manor, is now a farmhouse.

There are the remains of a pele tower, one of many in the area, at the west end of the house, which must have had four storeys. The earlier roof has been replaced by a modern pentroof. The tower was probably built late in the fourteenth century, and parts of the house may be of that time though they look slightly later. There is tradition that while the house was under construction a local lad from Troutbeck, Hugh Hird, passed by; noticing that ten men were struggling to lift a beam into place, he offered to do the job single-handed. Such was his strength that he raised the beam over his shoulders, it was thirty feet long and eighteen by twelve inches wide, and slid it into place. Hird gained the nickname of the 'Cork Lad of Kentmere'. It is said that he went down to London where his trials of strength earned him a considerable reputation, but his heart could not continue to take the strain and he collapsed and died at a young age pulling up trees by the roots.

On a personal note, Kentmere is fixed indelibly in my mind because of a picnic we once had at the head of the mere. My father was a great picnicker and we had in fact been to Kentmere on several previous occasions. There had been disasters at other places, like the 'bull picnic', where a bull had charged over the brow of a hill and we had made a quick exit over the wall, but Kentmere had always seemed a haven. However, on the day in question, it was during the summer holidays, two of my children in one of their games crawled too near a wasp's nest. The wasps went into a swift attack and the boys were so badly stung we had to rush them to the chemist's at Staveley. The 'wasp picnic' has stung us into Staveley, which is where we want to be next.

Staveley

Staveley is situated at the point where the River Gowan flows into the Kent and, as the main road from Kendal to Windermere passes right through the village, it is a familiar name to all who drive from the south to the Lake District. Some will have waited at times for the train to go by at the Staveley level-crossing, about a mile south of the village, or when passing through the main street will have noticed the grim inn sign of the Eagle and Child, and the mild-looking Duke William on the opposite side of the road.

The name, Staveley, means 'a wood or glade where staves

were cut'. The name is of English origin from *staef* meaning a rod or stave, and the Old English word for a wood or woodland clearing, *leah*. Originally a chapelry of Kendal Parish, Staveley was comprised of three townships: Over Staveley, Nether Staveley, and part of Hugill, 'the high ravine', situated northeast of the modern village, the region of Hugill Fell.

Staveley was at one time a market town. In 1281, William de Thweng was granted the right to hold a market on Fridays at his 'Manor of Staveley in Kendale and a 3 days fair on the eve, day, and morrow of St Luke the Evangelist'. The fair would have been held on the 17th, 18th and 19th of October. A few years later Sir William was also granted the right of free warren in Staveley, but, more importantly, he founded the Chapel of St Margaret which he endowed with land and arranged in his will for a suitable chaplain to be appointed at all times. I say 'suitable' because of this clause in the will: 'If any such chaplain shall become unfit by reason of any crime committed, or shall be incorrigible, he shall be utterly removed from the said chantry and another shall be called to his place.' There was, of course, a certain amount of self-interest in this, for the chief purpose in founding chantry chapels was to ensure that Masses were said for the repose of the soul of the founder; an 'incorrigible' chaplain could not be relied upon.

Thomas Machell also mentioned Staveley, which he described as 'a pretty village with a neat chapel and a level graveyard: there is a cross at the gates and a bridge nearby. The dedication of this chapel is not now known; but from this inscription round one of the bells, I take it to be St Margaret's chapel.' It is strange that there was nobody in Staveley at the time who could have confirmed Machell's supposition. Did anyone know? Even the chaplain, William Harrison, who showed Machell a piece of firestone found in Borrowdale Fells, did not know. Perhaps, as was fairly common at the time, he knew more about rocks than the Resurrection!

All that remains today of St Margaret's is the tower with one three-light window in which the small diamonds of glass have taken many well-aimed stones, and two small windows with very old-looking moulded arches beside the tiny bell openings. The tower certainly needs attention, and I found it almost impossible to read the War Memorial plaque above the door, though the door itself has a notice recalling a meeting which took place on 2nd of January, 1621. The High Constable of Staveley, James Smith, brought together a group from the townships ostensibly to inspect the bridge over the Kent, but the real purpose of the gathering was to draw up a protest against James I's plan to take over the Border estates, estates held in return for 'Border Service' under what was termed Border Tenant's Right. It was all a bit of a try-on by the King who felt that now England and Scotland were united under one throne the bargain no longer existed. It would be a good way of increasing the Crown Revenue. The result was that Smith and some hundred other men were indicted before the Court of Star Chamber in November, 1622, but the case dragged on, and it was not until Charles I had succeeded to the throne in 1625 that the tenants' case was given a satisfactory hearing, when judgment was found in their favour.

The decision not to renovate St Margaret's and to build another church was taken in 1864. The Manchester architect, J. S. Crowther, who carried out work also at Crosby Ravensworth and at St Mary's, Windermere, was asked to submit designs and the result was the building of St James's Church a little way up the road to Kentmere opposite the mills. There is nothing in Crowther's work to startle the eye, but Staveley does have one treasure in its east window. This is very beautiful and is the work of Sir Edward Burne-Jones and William Morris, the glass having been made at the Kelmscott Studio. The window was given by the widow of Daniel Harrison in memory of her husband in 1874. There are three lights altogether, and the centre light shows Christ on the cross with several typical Burne-Jones figures above, of which I noted the top one has the famous Burne-Jones face! The two outer lights are by Morris who has designed fine angels with a deep-blue background.

Staveley is worth visiting for this, and also because some of the earliest mills were situated in this part of the Kent Valley. There is evidence that there were at least six fulling-mills working in Cumberland and Westmorland before 1185, and that two of these, at Ulthwaite North, in Hugill, and Barley Bridge, Staveley, were in operation as early as 1135! At Barley Bridge, on the village side of the river, there was a fourteenth-century corn-mill; while on the far side Kentmere Limited is still in business near the spot where the early fulling-mill is thought to have stood. Water-power was used in the wool trade at Staveley until as late as 1971!

It was the considerable drop in height that the river gives, particularly in its early stages, that made it so ideal for milling; and on the Kent itself, and its tributaries, there were at one time or another as many as sixty mills in operation. Some of these were very old while others, as was the case of several mills in the town of Kendal itself, were built during the eighteenth century. The only mill still using water-power is the snuff-mill at Helsington, south of the town.

At Staveley there were probably as many as eight mills, of which two were associated with the lead-mines as smelting-mills; the others were either corn-mills, or in some way involved in the wool trade for spinning, bobbin-turning or fulling. On the Gowan, a very short stream, there were seven mills situated; this narrow river may be seen running parallel with the road, the A591, on the south side between Staveley and Ings.

Travellers on the A591, however, are usually moving so fast that they would be unlikely to notice much anyway, and to take this fast road between Windermere and Kendal means missing most besides; for by far the most attractive way to go from Staveley to Kendal is to take the road across Barley Bridge and follow the east side of the Kent as far as Burneside, taking in, if one has time, Cowan Head and Bowston; both great mill places, and well known for their being early paper-mills. Cowan Head was in operation in the eighteenth century and was owned at one time by Cornelius Nicholson until it became part of the much larger business the young James Cropper took over in 1845. Nicholson had opened a second paper-mill at Burneside in 1833; the year after which, as it happens, he published his *Annals of Kendal*! The mill was a thriving business that James Cropper was able to develop, so much so that the name Cropper has been inextricably linked with the village of Burneside since 1845. I am tempted to head the next section 'The Croppers of Burneside', but as Burneside is considerably older than the Croppers, I shall introduce them at the appropriate time.

Burneside

The Parish of Burneside consists of two townships, Strickland Ketel and Strickland Roger, which were originally both townships in Kendal Parish. Burneside, which seems to take its name from an early Norse settler called Brunulf, was formerly a small manor situated in Strickland Roger on a small hill near the junction of the Kent and the River Sprint; but it has superseded the other names in importance, and the church was situated there.

The ancient manor of Strickland, 'the land where stirks or young cattle were pastured', was divided in Norman times into two moieties, that is, it was divided down the middle, the word 'moiety' being derived from the Latin *medius*. In practice, the halves were often of a disproportionate size, as was the case here; Strickland Roger being some thousand acres or so the larger. In this Ketel was being generous, for it is thought to have been he, the grandson of Ivo de Tailbois, the first Lord of Kendal, who granted to a fellow Norman, Roger, the larger portion of land. Unfortunately nothing is known about Roger, and nothing either about Randolph, for there is a record of 1297 mentioning a Strickland Randolph, and there are several other references to it in the fourteenth century.

The larger part of the village of Burneside is situated in Strickland Ketel. St Oswald's Church, which was built in 1881, is the third church to occupy the site in a fairly short period of time. The Baptismal Register begins in 1717 when a church was built, and when another building was decided upon in 1826 a graveyard was added and so the Burial Register dates from that time. Prior to 1826 it would have been necessary to bear the dead to Kendal for burial.

St Oswald's was designed by C. J. Ferguson, the architect who also designed many churches in Cumberland including St Aidan's, Warwick Road, Carlisle, and two Westmorland churches at Middleton and Tebay. The most distinctive feature is probably the fine tower situated at the south-west of the church.

Burneside Hall, which is now a farmhouse, is reminiscent of the hall at Kentmere in that there is a fourteenth-century pele tower, though in a ruined state, very much in evidence. This was the defensive home of a family that took its name from the place, calling themselves Burneshead which was the earlier spelling. The hall is said to date back to the reign of Edward I. In 1290, Gilbert Burneshead, Under-Sheriff of Westmorland, lived there, and it was his daughter, Margaret, who by marriage passed the property to the Bellinghams. Margaret's husband, Richard Bellingham, was the first of several generations to occupy the hall until Sir Roger Bellingham was forced to sell up his estate during the reign of Henry III, and it was bought by Sir Thomas Clifford. However, Clifford sold it again very soon afterwards and it passed through many hands, until it was eventually bought by James Winstanley Cropper, of Summer How. One of the families who owned the hall were the Braithwaites, who had originated in Ambleside, so it was at Burneside Hall that Richard Braithwaite, the notorious 'Drunken Barnaby' or, as his schoolfellows would have it, 'Dapper Dick', was born in 1588.

Little is known of Braithwaite's early life beyond the fact that in 1604 at the age of sixteen he went up to Oriel College, Oxford, where, according to Wood's *Athenae Oxoniensis*, 'he avoided as much as he could the rough paths of logic and philosophy, and traced those smooth ones of poetry and Roman history, in which at length he did excel'. Braithwaite was to write the *Lives of the Roman Emperors*, and several other prose works which include *Essays on the Five Senses*, published in 1635, and two plays; but Braithwaite's verse is more interesting, and not particularly as verse, but for what it tells us about the Kendal of the time:

> Thence to Kendal, pure her state is,
> Prudent too her magistrate is;
> In whose charter to them granted
> Nothing but a Mayor wanted:
> Here it likes me to be dwelling,
> Bousing, loving stories telling.

These lines are from *Barnaby's Journal*, which describes several journeys to and from the North of England.

The period when Kendal had no mayor as Braithwaite mentions, dates the poem to before 1636 when Thomas Sleddall, who had been twice Alderman, was appointed 'first and moderne Maior of ye Borough of Kendal'. The year before this event,

Braithwaite had been prompted to write a poem on the Windermere ferry disaster of 19th of October, 1635. There had been great floods, the Kent had risen as high as the church vestry, and the Windermere ferryman, Thomas Miller, together with forty-seven men and women and nine horses were drowned when the ferry sank. It is possible that many of them were drunk at the time since they had attended a wedding, and perhaps that aroused 'Drunken Barnaby's' sympathy. As far as is known, there is only one copy of this poem in existence and this is lodged safely in the Bodleian Library at Oxford. As Braithwaite was undoubtedly a poet of sorts and wrote about Windermere it is not too extravagant to claim him as the first of the Lake Poets, one whom even De Quincey failed to mention!

Richard Braithwaite married twice; his first wife, Frances Lawson, bore him nine children. When she died in 1633 she was greatly mourned by her husband:

> Near Darlington was my dear darling borne
> Of noble house, which yet bears honour's form.

The Lawson home was at Nesham, near Darlington. Braithwaite remained a widower for six years and then remarried. His second wife was Mary Croft who came from Kirtlington, in Yorkshire. She bore him several more children, but it seems that on his marriage Braithwaite decided to leave his Westmorland home after allowing those of his tenants who wished it to buy their farms from his estate: he lived at Appleton, near Richmond, in Yorkshire, until his death in the May of 1673, and he was buried in the church at Catterick:

> Where I'll stay and end my journay,
> Till brave Barnaby returne-a.

Of the many mills situated along the course of the Kent, Cropper's paper-mill at Burneside is rightly considered the most important. As I have already said, James Cropper took over the business at Cowan Head in 1845, together with the mill at Burneside which had opened in 1833. A member of a Liverpool Quaker family, he had married into the Wakefield family, and was only twenty-two when he took over the business. However, he was quick to take two other able businessmen into partnership, William Blacklock and George McCorquodale; later, they were joined by John Bryce. In taking over the paper-mills James Cropper had been well informed of the plan to increase the flow of water to the many mills by constructing reservoirs, and damming near their sources the Rivers Kent, Mint and Sprint. In fact, Queen Victoria signed an Act of Parliament on 21st of July, 1845: 'An Act for making and Maintaining Reservoirs in the Parish of Kendal in the county of Westmorland.' Various surveys were carried out and eventually the Kentmere Head Reservoir was completed during the summer of 1848. The cost of the work had been £13,435, and was so far in excess of the estimate that the plans for the other reservoirs were dropped! The Act of Parliament had stipulated that the commissioners, who were, in effect, the mill-owners, could raise money for the work, and then levy a rate for themselves which would be based on each foot of fall used by each mill. The Croppers owned three mills, for a third had been opened at Bowston, in 1880, and they owned 51 feet of fall altogether. This was by far the greatest footage, and the result has been that as the other mills have either closed down or taken to using alternative means of power, James Cropper and Co. has become the virtual owner of the reservoir.

James Cropper died in 1900 and he had lived to see his paper-making business expand out of all recognition, though he was fortunately saved from the anguish of seeing the Burneside mill largely destroyed by fire in 1903. Today, with a member of his family at the helm, James Cropper and Co. is among the most important makers of coloured, strong paper and board in the world.

Whatever progress the Cropper family may make in the manufacturing of paper will be equally matched by one member of the family's ability to write on it, for Margaret Cropper was, to quote Norman Nicholson: 'the most important poet to come out of Westmorland since Wordsworth'.

Margaret Cropper

Margaret Beatrice Cropper had been born in 1886, the youngest but one of the five children of Charles James Cropper. Such was her humility, she considered herself to be the least talented of the family. However, her love of poetry had developed early, and she could remember her grandfather reading poems aloud. The family visited London at least once a year for a round of the theatres, and Margaret Cropper's first book, entitled simply *Poems*, was published in London by Elkin Matthews, in 1914. It contained several poems with a city theme.

Four collections of her poems were published before the outbreak of the Second World War, by which time Margaret Cropper had established herself as a poet of supreme skill, always technically sound, with a clear, individual voice, drawing her imagery chiefly from the Westmorland landscape. 'I wrote most plays for local people,' she once said. The second book, *The Broken Hearth-Stone* came out in 1926; to be followed three years later by *The Springing Well*, which included one of her best-loved poems, 'The Easy Yoke'. Margaret Cropper was a committed Christian who wrote many devotional poems and verse dramas to be performed in church, some of these were published by the SPCK.

In 1932 Constable brought out the first of the long narrative poems, 'Little Mary Crosbie'. This was a tale about an orphan girl fostered by old Susannah Winter at her cottage, Watcher's Gate. In this poem Margaret Cropper revealed her compassion for, and deep understanding of, the Westmorland folk and their dialect. In this she broke new ground, since instead of using what one might call 'folksy' spelling, and I think immediately of the poems Tennyson attempted in the Lincolnshire dialect, Margaret Cropper, by introducing a dialectal idiom or placing a dialect word in the right place, managed to give a convincing version of the Westmorland tone of speech.

Another narrative poem, 'The End of the Road' was published in 1933; the volume included several shorter poems, among which was 'Dorothy Wordsworth Wakes at Allan Bank' which Norman Nicholson chose for his *The Lake District Anthology*; and a poem I like very much, 'The Woodcock's Flight at Dusk':

> Hist, there he flies! You hear at first his sharp
> Scimitar note, and then the rhythmic croak,
> As he hurries, hurries, with a feverish wing-beat,
> On his tireless circle at twilight through the woods.

The woodcock at dusk in May . . . You hear him come
When the woods are deep in bluebells, and every breath
Is heavy with scent, and with the Spring languor:
He crosses them unlanguorous, hurrying, urgent.

The hoarse beat of his note, sinister sweet,
Stirs in my spirit like an elfin drum,
Summoning me once more to the hidden threshold,
Where I shall receive a draught of rare virtue,

That, mixed with my chill blood, shall quicken my being
Till my spirit, twitched awhile from my cumbered body,
Flies swiftly, passionately, through dim stretches,
Tuned to a mystic beat, that hastens, and is gone.

To my mind, though, the best of the long, narrative poems was
'Anthony Broom', which came out in 1937. Margaret Cropper
once told me that one of the blessings of her having lived much of
her life on her own, which was true till her later years, was that
she had been able to write these comparatively long poems.
Ironically, it is very likely because they are long and demand
concentrated reading that they are not better known, but the
reward is rich, and these poems must surely become essential
for those who love the history and traditions of English country
life. 'You have to know a place pretty well to write poetry about
it,' Margaret Cropper once said. Few people can have known
Westmorland better.

Norman Nicholson has written of Margaret Cropper's work:
'It belongs to the same tradition as poets such as Hardy, Edward
Thomas and Wilfred Owen, who, in their quiet, unspectacular
way helped to bring about a revolution in the language of poetry
almost as effectively as did the more spectacular impact of Eliot
and Pound.' However, it was the impact of Eliot and Pound and
their followers which accounted for Margaret Cropper's work
being known to so few, but I have a hunch that if some wise
publisher were to bring out an edition of her poems, her reputation would grow far beyond anything she might have imagined
in her lifetime.

The *Collected Poems*, published in 1958 and now, sadly, out of
print, brought together the long poems and many of the shorter
ones; but there were many representative poems missing; besides, Margaret Cropper continued to write well into her old age,

in fact, one or two of her poems about the experience of being old were included in her last book, *Something and Everything* which Abbot Hall Art Gallery published in 1978. At this time the poet's home was Laurel Cottage in Burneside where she continued to live until a few weeks before her death on 27th of September, 1980. Among her last poems was this beautiful one 'I'll hold your hand' written at Laurel Cottage:

> They were unkind steps, no rail for the old and shaken,
> And there they lay. Most days, on my way home,
> They brought me to a stand – a halting moment;
> 'If you should fall,' they said, 'if you should fall.'
> I was standing feeling rather fearful and old,
> When I heard a voice behind me, a childish voice,
> Almost too soft to be heard, and into my hand
> A very small hand came, peacefully holding mine.
> It was such a small hand, a six-year-old hand perhaps,
> Holding my withered fingers in innocent grasp;
> It was matched by the sweetest voice, and the confident message:
> 'I'll hold your hand till you get down those steps.'
> I don't think I could have fallen after that;
> It would have been blasphemy to think of falling;
> So step by step I went hopefully to the road.
> I dared then to look round, but the child had vanished;
> I never saw her – but something stirred in me,
> Someone had come, someone had come to help me.

I do not think that Margaret Cropper ever worried much about literary success. If anything, she was probably better known for the few biographical books she wrote than for her poems. She wrote a life of Evelyn Underhill who had been a personal friend, and three volumes of short biographical sketches of Anglican 'saints', of the seventeenth, eighteenth and nineteenth centuries, *Flame Touches Flame*, *Sparks Among the Stubble* and *Shining Lights*, the last of which included essays on Christina Rossetti and Mother Cecile of Grahamstown.

As to her poems, Sir John Betjeman wrote to me recently: 'I agree with you about Margaret Cropper. The more people read her, the more people will enjoy her.'

Goat Scar and Raven Crag, Longsleddale

But I didn't want anything new,
Only primroses growing where they always grew,
No, I didn't want anything new,

And I didn't want anything grand,
Only curlews calling over the tufted land,
No, I didn't want anything grand.

I only wanted to go
To the fields to see things grow,
And to wander to and fro –

On what better note could we leave Burneside than that!

Castle Hill from Kendal Green

2

A Tale of Two Rivers

Of Westmorland the Muse now sings.
Michael Drayton

By the time the Kent reaches the town of Kendal its waters have been multiplied greatly by several smaller becks and rivers that have flowed into it. The River Gowan was the first of any size, meeting the Kent at Staveley; but as attractive as the little Gowan might be it offers nothing to compare with the two rivers I intend now to consider, the Sprint and the Mint.

The River Sprint rises high on the fells about a mile south of Haweswater. From the slopes of Adam Seat it begins as Wren Gill flowing swiftly between Raven Crag and Goat Scar on its western side, the Buckbarrow Crag on the east. Continuing in a south-easterly direction it enters Longsleddale which, as its name suggests, is a long, deep valley, though the 'dale' part of the name is one of those unnecessary additions found in several Westmorland names, since *slead* was the Old English word for a valley. The most often quoted repetitions of this sort are Lake Windermere, where 'Lake' and 'mere' are synonymous, and the Howgill Fells where both *howe* and *fell* were Old Norse words for a hill. While speaking of names, perhaps I should point out that Goat Scar has nothing to do with goats, but derives its name from another Norse word, *goltr*, which meant a wild boar, an example to remind us that in the origins of place-names sensible guesses are often wide of the mark.

The upper reaches of the Sprint may only be approached on foot, but the track is not difficult going from Sadgill, where there is an early packhorse bridge across the stream. The Sprint takes the waters of Stockdale Beck about a mile south of Sadgill, 'the ravine with pastureland' and not in the least sad, and continues

34

south-eastwards, passing Swinklebank, 'the bank of the swine-spring', presumably a watering place for the swine that foraged for the beech-mast in the forests. Longsleddale is still more wooded than most of the valleys in the vicinity, and this is particularly noticeable behind Ubarrow Hall.

Although there are several well-built seventeenth-century farms on either side of the river, Ubarrow Hall is one of the more interesting houses in the valley. Ubarrow is really Yewbarrow, and the hall is mentioned in Nicholson and Burn as 'the most considerable house in the dale'. 'Ubery Hall', as they call it, 'has an ancient tower and the walls two yards thick.' I must confess that it was a few minutes before I realized that what looks like a tall barn was the remains of a pele tower, but soon all became plain. The tower has been chopped off at the top and a gabled roof added. The house, not a large one, adjoining the tower is of the seventeenth century. Little is known of the tower's history beyond the fact that it was granted to Robert de Leyburne, a member of the distinguished Skelsmergh family, about which I shall have more to say in a moment, and that it passed from the Leyburnes to the Harringtons sometime during the reign of Henry III. The Harringtons seem to have held on to it, and during the reign of Henry VIII they were paying a 'free' rent of one shilling to the Parrs of Kendal Castle.

Longsleddale was one of the chapelries of Kendal Parish: there were twenty-four altogether. It is fairly certain that there would have been a small chapel in the valley in mediaeval times, for the community was active in the wool industry by the end of the thirteenth century. In 1297 there was a fulling-mill at Sadgill which implies that Longsleddale like the other Kendal townships was busily employed. Although the dead would have been taken to the parish church in Kendal for burial, it is reasonable to suppose that they would not have had to travel so far to Mass. It is known that a chapel was rebuilt and a graveyard consecrated in 1712, but the church's treasure of an Elizabethan chalice and paten, made of London silver in 1571, is good evidence that there was a flourishing church at the time. The present building, dedicated to the Virgin Mary, was completed in 1863, and is one of the churches of the United Benefice of Skelsmergh, Selside and Longsleddale.

Near the church stands the old school, though it has long been closed as a school. The last days of the children's occupation has been well described in *The School in the Fells*, a short book by the last mistress to teach there, Olwen Harris. Miss Harris arrived in Longsleddale in 1940, and remained with the children until they were moved to Selside, in 1942, to which they were taken each day by taxi.

The church and school are on the chief road running parallel with the river on the eastern side of the valley, but there was a packhorse track along the western side also which passed Kilnstone Farm, a sixteenth-century building that was used in the days of the packhorse trains as an inn.

Longsleddale comes to an end at Garnett Bridge, a small hamlet where once two mills were at work, the last closing soon after the First World War. Near this hidden little place the Sprint reaches its most easterly point before turning due south for a while then continuing south-westwards towards Burneside, passing Garth Row, Oakbank and Sprint Mill on the way.

There are many who consider Longsleddale, the valley of the lively Sprint, the 'running or bounding river', to be the loveliest in Westmorland. It made a deep impression on the novelist Mrs Humphrey Ward; in *Robert Elsmere* Longsleddale becomes the 'Long Whindale' of the opening scenes where the author uses impressions drawn from memories of a drive along the valley two years before the novel was completed in 1887. As the author recalled in *A Writer's Recollections*:

> In 1885, in March some friends drove me up the remote Westmorland valley of Long Sleddale, at a moment when the blackthorn made the lines white along the lanes; and from that day onward the early chapters of *Robert Elsmere* began to shape themselves in my mind.

It is easy to see how Sleddale became 'Whindale' when Whinfell was so close at hand, though in her later novel, *Helbeck of Bannisdale*, Mrs Humphrey Ward was less cautious. It would be to Bannisdale that we would go next were I to allow the Mint to follow the Sprint, but sunny Selside must come between!

Selside
Across the main road, the A6, from Kendal to Penrith, and almost opposite the turning down to Garnett Bridge, a narrow

lane leads to Selside, another small hamlet with a church and fine old hall. Selside was always known as Selside-with-Whitwell, and like Longsleddale it was one of the Kendal chapelries situated between the Sprint and the Mint and extending from four and a half to six and a half miles north-by-east of Kendal Town; an area surrounded on the northern and eastern sides by high fells but itself occupying more gentle hills. Selside Hall is one of the best old houses in the district and was built largely for defence in the fourteenth century by a family that took its name, de Selside, from the place, as was the normal practice. However, by the time of Edward I the property had passed to the Thornburghs, a family of Norman origin that had been granted estates in Yorkshire, and took their name from the Manor of Thornburgh in that county. The first member of this new family to own Selside was Roland de Thornburgh who was also granted land by the Abbot of Shap in the area. Shap Abbey was in possession of most of Longsleddale, and it was probably a shrewd move on the part of the abbot to gain Thornburgh's support in return for land close to his home. It is known that in 1279 Roland de Thornburgh received more abbey land in Reagill and Mauld's Meaburn in the Appleby Barony, and a further grant of land in Sleddale in 1291. Gradually the family was able to control the whole manor of Selside together with considerable areas of Sleddale, Whinfell and Skelsmergh.

There is an interesting record of 1419 when Shap Abbey leased land to the Thornburghs on the condition that 'If by chance there should be an invasion of the Scots and any of the property should be burned or destroyed, then Roland de Thornburgh shall be released of that portion of service appertaining to the property destroyed.' This makes the relationship between the family and the abbey clear, although the number of Rolands among the generations of Thornburghs can lead to confusion. This particular Roland had been involved in a scandal in 1404 when he had, at the instigation it seems of Thomas Warcop of Lammerside Castle, carried off the young nine-year-old Margaret de Sandford against her will and married her to Warcop's son. Sir Robert de Leyburne, of Skelsmergh, who was a relative of the girl, petitioned Parliament for justice to be brought against Thornburgh since threats had been made against anyone who tried to interfere in the matter. Not surprisingly, the

Chief Justice, William Gascoign, brought against Thornburgh and young Margaret was allowed to live with the Leyburnes. This incident is not an isolated one in the history of this family, for in 1443 a William Thornburgh, Roland's son, was involved in the murder of Robert de Crackenthorpe, a local Justice of the Peace, though when the trial was heard at Appleby William's younger brothers were accused and found guilty. However, they were later acquitted when they appealed and managed to prove that at the time of the murder they were in Calais on the King's business. There was something fishy about the whole case, but it is not known how William Thornburgh managed to 'get away with it'.

The Thornburghs were connected by marriage to many of the important local families, and William Thornburgh's son, also called William, was married twice, first to Cecily Curwen, and then to Thomasine Bellingham. This latter match brought more valuable property into the family, and a higher status, for the Bellinghams were particularly important at the time. Lady Thomasine came to Selside in 1537. Only three years later she would have heard that Shap Abbey had been forcibly closed down in the middle of January, and all the monks, some of whom were members of local families, would now have to seek other refuge and employment. The injustice of it all may have helped to strengthen the resolve of families like the Thornburghs, for it is a remarkable fact that several important families in the district held out in support of the Old Religion through thick and thin, and of these the Thornburghs were among the staunchest defenders of the Faith.

I shall have more to tell of these families when I come to the extraordinary Leyburnes of Skelsmergh, but before leaving Selside suffice it to say that in order to pay the crippling recusancy fines the Thornburghs were obliged to sell up all their estates. Little more than the hall remained when the last of the family to dwell at Selside, Mary Thornburgh, married Ralph Riddell, of Cheesburn Grange, in Northumberland, in 1774. After this the house became the property of the Wilsons.

St Thomas's Church is situated a few hundred yards north-east of the hall on a small hill. Its most distinctive feature is the tower which is quite unlike any other church in the area, being particularly broad and forming part of the nave inside the church. This tower was an addition to the church, made in 1894, but the main part of the building was erected in 1838. This stands on the site of an earlier eighteenth-century chapel on land the Thornburghs donated, in 1709, on condition that their own private chapel at the hall could be used openly for the celebration of the Catholic Mass. This condition was granted, which is remarkable considering the time.

The River Mint

The Mint rises as Banniside Beck on the southern slopes of Banniside Fell. It flows swiftly down its steep-sided valley leaving the area of Fawcett Forest high up on the eastern side. By Thorn Cottage and Lowbridge House it passes beneath the A6 and on till near Whelpside, swelled by the waters of several smaller streams, it takes a southerly course through the small township of Patton. Then about a mile or so west of Grayrigg swings westwards by Mealbank to meet the Kent on the northern edges of Kendal. A modern industrial estate is situated near the confluence of the two rivers in an area for long known as Mintsfeet.

As we have seen in the case of the origin of the Kent's name, the names of rivers are usually very old, and this is certainly true of the Mint. The name has been written in several forms, the modern spelling being first recorded in the twelfth century; but 'Mimmet' and 'Mimed' are among the other spellings and these seem to relate to the Sanskrit *mimati*, meaning to bleat or cry. The name probably is meant to imply something like 'the noisy river'. One thing is certain, it has nothing to do with any wild mint that might be found growing beside it!

The large area of Fawcett Forest at one time took in parts of Shap and Orton Parishes besides the north-eastern part of the Parish of Kendal. The name Fawcett means the 'many-coloured hillside' from the Old English *fag* and *side*, and the region was designated a 'forest' which means that it was set aside as a hunting ground for the lord of the barony and there were heavy penalties attaching to any poaching. The manor was granted to the Abbot of Byland Abbey, in Yorkshire, by William de Lancaster, the second of that name, in the latter part of the twelfth century. In 1251, the Abbot brought a case against several

huntsmen, for hunting, we may assume, was what they were up
to. The record reads:

> 'The Abbot of Byland complained against Peter de Brus, Ralph de
> Eynecurt, Gilbert de Lancaster, Alan, son of Richard de Coupland,
> Nicholas in the forest of Banandesdale, Ralph the forester, Richard
> Buman, Thomas Godman and Richard de Lowriche for entering his
> land.'

One imagines that the prey ran into the abbey lands and the
chase continued beyond the confines of the forest, for they seem
rather a respectable group of gentlemen to have been poachers,
though I imagine Ralph the forester might have helped himself
to the odd wild boar or stag had he wanted to without anyone
knowing much about it! The early spelling of Bannisdale as
Banandesdale, 'the forbidden dale', is interesting, but if anyone
is thinking the group might fit the tune of 'Widecombe Fair', I
have tried it and failed.

Byland Abbey continued to hold the manor until the monastery was dissolved, and it was soon snapped up by Alan Bellingham, one of those who became rich on abbey lands and much else
in the Kendal region.

Whinfell
Whinfell, 'the hill overgrown with whins or gorse', is situated
east of Fawcett Forest and the Mint Valley. It is really a ridge of
hills that separates that valley from Borrowdale, an attractive dale that drops down towards the Howgills where Borrow Beck meets the Lune near Low Borrow Bridge, and
where the Romans had a station on the southern side of the
stream.

Borrowdale, which must not be mistaken for its better-known
brother in the Lake District, is a good valley for walkers, but so
is the Whinfell Ridge which includes the tops of Ashstead Fell,
Mabbin Crag, Castle Fell, Whinfell Beacon and Grayrigg Common. The beacon is known even by those who do not know its
name, for there is a Post Office Radio Repeater Station perched
near the summit. Some people have objected strongly to its
presence, but I do not mind it in the least.

Whinfell Beacon, as the name suggests, was one of the heights from which a warning could be given of an impending raid, giving the local inhabitants a little time to barricade themselves inside their pele towers. The beacon is not, however, the highest point on the Ridge; it stands 1,544 feet above sea-level which means that Mabbin Crag is some twenty-six feet higher, but Grayrigg Common is higher still at 1,619 feet. The view from Whinfell is magnificent on a clear day: to the south the Kent Estuary and Morecambe Bay, and to the west the mountains of the Lake District; Black Combe, some thirty miles away, the Coniston Fells, Scafell, Great Gable and the dollops of the Langdale Pikes. Yet on certain days one can see nothing, only greyness, though I hasten to add that Grayrigg, 'the grey ridge', is not always grey.

Grayrigg
This small village is situated on a small area of grey carboniferous limestone; through it the A685 passes on its way between Kendal and Tebay where it continues towards Kirkby Stephen, Brough and the A66, the Stainmore road. I have driven along that road so many times and in so many moods that I have often passed through Grayrigg without noticing it. 'Have we been through Grayrigg yet?' I might say to a passenger. This is not because Grayrigg lacks interest, it is simply that I tend to be behind time always, and I am often thinking of other things. I hope that constitutes 'due care and attention'. No, approached from any other road, the Whinfell road, for instance, Grayrigg Church tower becomes another beacon against the skyline, or from the south, along the road railway passengers must have taken after alighting at Grayrigg Station, long since closed down, the village becomes a place to arrive at rather than to pass through.

Once a chapelry of Kendal Parish, Grayrigg included the townships of Docker, Lamrigg, and Whinfell. Another township, Dillicar, was attached to Grayrigg for ecclesiastical purposes, although it was, as we shall see, part of the Lonsdale Ward. Today Grayrigg is linked with Old and New Hutton and is what is called a 'plurality', which sounds a little like the plague.

As the village was some distance from the parish church in Kendal, Grayrigg had its own chapel in mediaeval times, and unlike Longsleddale there is a record of 1467 in existence which states that the people of Grayrigg were licensed to hear divine service in their own chapel. The present church, St John's, was rebuilt by subscription in 1838, but the work seems to have been poorly executed since the walls of the tower gave way only thirty years later and had to be rebuilt at a cost of £700, about half the cost of the original building altogether!

The Manor of Grayrigg was given by William de Lancaster, the first of that name, with the hand of his daughter, Agnes, in marriage to Alexander de Windsore, and the manor remained in the de Windsore family for many generations until it passed by marriage to the Duckets, the family with whom Grayrigg is most associated. There is an interesting record of the year 1385 to the effect that:

> William de Windsore, Lieutenant of Ireland, Knight, the husband of Alice de Perers, the 'Lady of the Sun', the famous Court Beauty of the latter years of King Edward III, died without issue in 1385, when it was found by inquest taken in London that his sisters, Isabella, aged 38, Christina, wife of Sir William Morieux, aged 34, and Margaret or Margery, wife of John Ducket, aged 32, were his heirs.

It was through Margaret or Margery that the Duckets had come to Westmorland, for she had married John Ducket, a young squire from Fillingham, in Lincolnshire.

The Ducket family home was Grayrigg Hall, a large house largely demolished at the beginning of this century, though part of it remains as a farmhouse. It was situated about a mile north of the village on the Whinfell road, and was described as 'an embattled structure'. When the last member of the family to own the hall, Anthony Ducket, sold it to Sir John Lowther, in 1695, it had already begun to deteriorate badly, and the lead, timber and other moveables of this fine quadrangular house were moved to Lowther.

At the Kendal end of the village, near the church, there is a row of six almshouses endowed by Miss Mary Rowlandson and her brothers for 'The aged and indigent' of the parish in 1868; and it is to Miss Rowlandson that the east window of the church is dedicated, for she had been born and brought up in the village before moving to Akay Lodge, Sedbergh.

There is still a lively little school at Grayrigg, situated on the south side of the road. This is an important part of village life, and there has been a school there since the first was founded, in 1818, for boys only, though the school became a mixed establishment in 1897.

It was at a small house in Grayrigg that a young boy from Orton, George Whitehead, attended his first Quaker meeting in 1652. The house was named Sunny Bank and it was the home of an ex-army captain called Henry Ward. Whitehead was barely sixteen; he experienced 'a great work of the Power of the Lord', something that changed his life so radically that he became the great Quaker missionary, the 'Quaker Moses', enduring incredible hardships, insults and frequent imprisonments before his death, in 1723. It was also in the Chapelry of Grayrigg at a house in the fells called Todthorne, now no longer standing, that another famous Quaker, Francis Howgill, was born, and both he and George Whitehead were present when George Fox preached in the parlour of Sunny Bank.

Lambrigg and Docker

Lambrigg and Docker Fells are situated due south of Grayrigg. They are not very high hills, but in attractive country. The fells either gave their names to or took them from the two small townships of Lambrigg and Docker. Lambrigg will need no explanation, but Docker seems to be derived from two Old Norse words, *dokk* and *erg*, the latter we shall meet several times. It meant a dairy-farm, and is to be found in Skelsmergh, Sizergh, Manzergh and Mansergh, where it is easily recognized, but also it is hidden in Winder and, as here, in Docker. The *dokk* part meant a hollow or valley, so the name simply means something like 'the dairy-farm in the valley'.

Docker, a small manor in its own right, was granted by William de Lancaster to the leper hospital of St Leonard's, York (formerly called St Peter's), which ran a house in Scalthwaiterigg. This was situated a little to the east of Benson Knott, the highest point of Hay Fell which separates Scalthwaiterigg from Docker.

The hospital had been endowed by several of the early Lords of Kendal including the third, Lord Ketel, who had given lands in the Kirkby Lonsdale area, but it was William de Lancaster, the fifth lord, who granted Docker to the monks, a grant that was later confirmed by Gilbert Fitz-Reinfred, the husband of William's granddaughter. Fitz-Reinfred, who had been given vast acres of forest in Westmorland, Kendal and Furness by Richard I, made certain concessions to the monks, allowing them to let their horses and hogs roam free in the forest area, provided the men who tended them did not carry bows and arrows or use dogs. The reasons for this are obvious, but another concession shows how the lord cared for the monks' welfare, no doubt conscious of the good work they were doing, for he ordered that:

> If their cattle should stray out of the granted limits into the forest, they should be driven back quietly and without hurt or damage to the brethren of the said hospital.

On the outskirts of Kendal, on the Brough road, there is a farm known as Spital, in Scalthwaiterigg, 'the ridge with a clearing-shed or shieling'. This, of course, takes its name from the hospital, though I am not suggesting that the leper house was on that site.

It was the fact that Fitz-Reinfred owned land in Lambrigg that was to clear up a certain misunderstanding as to the real meaning of the word 'Westmorland'. We have seen that the eastern part of the county was the Barony of Westmorland, but it was once thought that the name meant something like 'the land of the western meres', where the 'meres' meant the Lakes. However, the *Anglo-Saxon Chronicle* refers to 'Westmoringa-land', by which the scribe means the 'people of the western moors'. As I have argued elsewhere the original Westmoringas were the people who settled along the reaches of the Upper Eden Valley and the Eden's tributaries, and we know this because of Lambrigg. Fitz-Reinfred in a document in which he speaks of the boundaries of lands he owned in Lambrigg refers to 'the great way which comes from Westmeriland'. For a moment it looks as though the 'meres' might be there, but the document makes it clear that lands to the east are meant. 'Westmorland', then, barony and all, was the land east of Lambrigg!

Patton

On the northern slopes of Lambrigg and Docker Fells several
small streams converge to form Flodder and Thrushgill Becks
which, flowing in a northerly direction, meet the Mint, the river
we had almost forgotten as we dealt with 'higher things'. The
Mint has come due south by Mozergh House, where nearby
there was once a mill, and Whinfell Tarn, beside which a narrow
road rambles parallel with the river passing the tarn on the
eastern side and a farmhouse called Borrans. Then, soon after
Haveriggs, the road crosses over the Mint at Patton Bridge to
Patton, once a township of the Selside Chapelry, whose name
means the 'farmstead with a track or path'. Presumably this was
some well-known track, which makes me think it must have
been the old Roman road from Natland to Low Borrow Bridge
which is thought to have crossed Whinfell Common, and may
have forded the Mint at two places; Laverock Bridge in Scalthwaiterigg, and Patton Bridge.

At Patton there is a small group of houses, and nearby a fairly
large house, Shaw End, built in the last century near a small
bend in the river. Soon the Mint plunges down a weir, a
reminder that there are several mills on this stretch of the river.
More were situated in the next little place, Mealbank, the
'coloured bank', where there are some modern houses together
with several older buildings, some of which were former mills. If
Mealbank is approached from Patton Bridge, Patton Hall will
be seen on the south side of the road. The road leads on to
Laverock Bridge, literally, 'the bridge of the lark', but Laverock
is probably derived from a surname here. Not far from the
bridge a short drive leads up to a strange-looking house, with an
even stranger history, called Dodding Green. The house takes
its name from a rich Kendal shearman, William Dodding, who
in the fourteenth century bought land from the Leyburne family
and built himself a house. The Doddings by marrying wisely
soon became connected with several local families and, during
the reign of Queen Elizabeth, a William Dodding became Chief
Clerk of the Crown in Kendal. William's son, Myles Dodding,
moved up to London where he seems to have curried favour with
the Queen who granted him all the lands that had once been
held by St Leonard's Hospital; and through his marriage with
Margaret Sandys, whose family had bought the priory at Conis-

head, Myles Dodding ended up an exceedingly rich man owning the priory and all its lands, since Margaret had no brothers.

Myles's own brother, however, had remained at home and married another Margaret, Margaret Thornburgh, of Selside Hall, and had eventually moved to near Penrith. Dodding Green was sold up and bought by the Braithwaites, of Burneside, and it remained in the family until Sir Thomas Braithwaite's widow sold the house to Robert Stephenson, in 1687. Braithwaite had died in York Castle, where he had been imprisoned for recusancy and contracted gaol fever. In order to assist Dame Alice Braithwaite, Stephenson and his family had moved into the house some years earlier, and it is with the Stephensons that Dodding Green is most associated, for Robert Stephenson being an ardent Catholic made his house the centre of the missionary activity in the district, fitting trap-doors and building priestholes so that at any moment a speedy exit could be made. The strange thing about all this was the good will Stephenson received from all who knew him, Protestants and Catholics alike. When a charge was eventually brought against him for harbouring priests, nobody was prepared to come forward to give evidence against him, and the case was dropped, although his activities were known by everyone.

One of the great sadnesses of Stephenson's life was that none of his children lived beyond their teens, and there was no one to inherit his estate. Perhaps this was the main reason why he decided to leave all to the maintaining of a priest at Dodding Green in perpetuity. This was something that began during the last years of his life, and from 1714 the first resident priest, Father Thomas Royden, administered the sacraments to the ageing benefactor. Stephenson died in 1723 and was buried in Kendal parish churchyard. It was not until 1791 that the first Catholic Relief Act was passed, but from the time Father Royden took up residence at Dodding Green, there was, apart from a very short period, a priest in residence, and so there is even today. The history of Dodding during the eighteenth and nineteenth centuries is of great interest, and those who wish to know more will find it finely described in *The Story of Skelsmergh* written by Sister Agnes in 1949. The mention of Skelsmergh brings us to the last stage of this pilgrimage in the land of the Sprint and the Mint.

Skelsmergh

Skelsmergh was one of the Kendal townships, so was not a chapelry, though in 1871 it became a parish in its own right taking in the three townships of Patton, Scalthwaiterigg-Hay, and Hutton-in-the-Hay, the last two both being situated in the 'hay' or hunting-ground of Kendal Castle. In the same year St John the Baptist's was built from designs by the Kendal architect Joseph Birtley in the Early English style. By choosing this simple style Birtley, who was later to design St John's Church at Beckermet in Cumberland, produced an attractive little church with a small bellcote of the type so familiar in the district.

Skelsmergh, which is not a village but a wide area of farmland, takes its name from one of the Norse settlers, Skaldmar, though he would have written it 'Skjaldmer'. This man may have given his name to Skelmersdale in Lancashire, and Skelmanthorpe in West Yorkshire, if, indeed, it was the same man. The Norsemen may have come into the area like the Anglians, across the Pennines and not so much as warriers but settlers, having already decided to remain in England after arriving in the east; or they may have come as plunderers sailing into Morecambe Bay and up the Kent Estuary having crossed from Ireland! Whichever way they came they made a lasting impression, for not only are many places named after individual Norsemen, but literally hundreds of place-names contain Norse elements. Some familiar words in the Westmorland dialect are exclusively Norse: words like 'beck', 'dale', 'fell', 'garth', 'tarn', and 'thwaite', meaning a clearing; but literally thousands of words were adopted where the Anglo-Saxon or English word was almost identical with the Norse. The word 'tun', for instance, found in Hutton and Patton was common to both languages, as was the 'rigg' in Grayrigg and Lambrigg, which meant a ridge or cultivated piece of ground. At Skelsmergh, it seems, Skaldmar had a dairy-farm, and what more does one needs to know than that?

Skelsmergh Hall was the home of the Leyburne family for several hundred years, though they also owned Cunswick Hall on the opposite side of Kendal. The manor had been granted to Robert de Leyburne in 1241, a member of a family that originated in Wensleydale taking the name of the Manor of Leyburn soon after the Norman Conquest. How the Leyburnes came to the Kendal area is of interest. A Roger de Leyburne had accompanied Richard I to the Holy Land on the Third Crusade, and on his return had married the daughter of the Baron of Kent. There is a village named after him near Maidstone to this day. Roger's son, another Roger, was thought a suitable bridegroom for Idonea, the younger daughter of Robert de Vipont, of this far northern county. It was all the scheme of King John, for de Vipont had died leaving no male heir and the estate reverted to the Crown. The King chose for Idonea's elder sister a young Herefordshire nobleman called Roger de Clifford, hence it was through these two girls that the famous families of Clifford and Leyburne came to be in Westmorland.

Sadly, Idonea died very soon after her marriage having born no children, so her estate and vast fortune reverted to her sister, Isabella, which is how the Clifford estates came to be so large. It is thought that on the death of his wife Roger de Leyburne remained in the county, and that it was he who built Cunswick Hall. He certainly married again, and it was to his eldest son, Robert, that the Manor of Skelsmergh was granted, in return for which he presented his overlord with a pair of gilt spurs each year.

The Leyburnes remained an important family in the county. In 1304 Sir Nicholas de Leyburne was Knight of the Shire, as was his descendant, Sir Robert de Leyburne, who lived a hundred years later. Sir Richard de Leyburne, an ancestor of Katherine Parr, became Admiral of the Western Seas in 1316 until his death when the position was taken by his younger brother, Sir Robert de Leyburne, who was married to Sarah de Harcla of Hartley Castle, near Kirkby Stephen. Sarah was the sister of Sir Andrew de Harcla, who was executed for failing to resist Robert Bruce's invasion of the North, in 1323.

It seemed that fortune favoured the Leyburnes just as it did the Cliffords, but the life of James Leyburne, who was born in 1490, saw a great change brought about in the family's position, although, as we shall see, it was the beginning of a different kind of success.

Sir James Leyburne had been on familiar terms with Henry VIII, who seems to have thought highly of him. At a time when Sir James had been ill, as he later informed Thomas Cromwell,

The upper reaches of the River Sprint, Longsleddale

the King's anxious letters had brought him much comfort. It was at York, in 1529, that the King knighted him in the Guild Hall.

In the matter of the Pilgrimage of Grace Sir James Leyburne supported the King while most northerners did not. On the 8th of October, 1536, Sir Thomas Wharton reported to Cromwell: 'Sir James Leyburne has been very diligent in the King's service upon the Western Marches. He dwells in the country of Kendal, the inhabitants whereof be very troublous.' Troublous the people of Kendal remained, for in the following year three hundred members of the congregation of Kendal Parish Church threatened to throw the minister, Sir Robert Applegarthe, into the Kent because he refused to pray for the Pope! Similar scenes were witnessed in Brough and Kirkby Stephen, and these threats on the part of the people against ministers who tried to force new religious practices upon them were at the time successful. Soon Cromwell was informed that the old priest in Kendal had returned and was praying for the Pope as before. What turned Sir James Leyburne's mind against the King ultimately was the terrible cruelty inflicted upon the people after the suppression of the revolt, which is known collectively as the Pilgrimage of Grace: the sight of townsmen and villagers hanging in chains to die, their bodies left to the elements, to be picked at by ravens and crows. This was enough: by 1539, the Earl of Derby informed the King that Sir James Leyburne had 'Sworn himself a Papist'.

Sir James died in 1548, a year after the King he had tried loyally to serve. In order to pay the heavy fines that were inflicted on him he had to sell part of his estate, but in his will he remembered the people of Skelsmergh, leaving them the tithes of three harvests after his death or the value of these in money, 'besides a dinner on a Sunday for five poor men or if they missed the meal they were to receive a penny each'. In return Sir James Leyburne asked the people of Skelsmergh to pray for his soul, and for those of his parents.

The Leyburnes possessed Skelsmergh Hall, the house they had built in the thirteenth century, but which they altered and extended several times during their four-hundred-year occupation. In 1715 the estate was forfeited to the Crown because of John Leyburne's support for the Jacobite Rebellion of that year,

Holy Trinity Church, Kendal

but although the family was deprived of property it was by no means the end of their influence, as we shall see when we come to their other home at Cunswick Hall.

3

Kendal Kirkland

Thence to Kirkland, thence to Kendal
I did that which men call spend-all
Richard Braithwaite

The older part of Kendal Town is Kirkland situated on the west bank of the Kent near a point where a small stream, Blind Beck, flows from the western fellside down to the larger river. Here, as the name implies, the first church has built, sometime during the ninth century. Yet, as old as Kirkland might be, it was not the first part of the town to be settled. Several hundred years earlier, when the Romans chose an ideal site by a 'crook' in the river for a military camp, they would have found small native settlements already in the vicinity. These were usually set fairly high on the hills, and here there was one on Sizergh Fell. The Roman camp, with the Kent forming a wide ditch around three-quarters of the site, was a little to the south of the land on which Kendal would begin, but, nevertheless, the town owes its origin to the Romans. It was the sensible practice of the Roman commanders to place watch-camps in strategic positions around the main fort and so it is not surprising to find at Kendal two such sites situated on either side of the river. These were on Castle Hill, on the eastern side where the Normans would later build in stone, and Castle Howe to the west. Such positions would remain useful forts even after the Roman Occupation, and in many cases they were taken over by the natives. There was certainly some kind of wooden castle at Kendal before Norman times, but it was the Normans who saw that stronger defences were built. On the Howe, or hill, they developed a motte-and-bailey castle which, although not as impressive as some in the district, is worth exploring.

While speaking of Castle Howe it is perhaps worth mentioning that on the motte, that is, the taller mound, a monument was erected in 1788 to commemorate the centenary of what is known in history as the Glorious Revolution, when the Stuart king, James II, was forced to abdicate in favour of his son-in-law, William of Orange. The monument is inscribed with the short phrase 'Sacred of Liberty', words which in 1795 caught the eye of Ann Radcliffe, the author of *The Mysteries of Udolpho* and other early horror novels, when she visited Kendal:

> At a time when the memory of that Revolution is reviled and the praises of liberty itself endeavoured to be suppressed by the artifice of imputing to it the crimes of anarchy, it was impossible to omit any act of veneration to the blessings of this event. Being thus led to ascend the hill, we had a view of the country over which it presides: a scene, simple, great and free, as the spirit revered amidst it!

Certainly the view Mrs Radcliffe saw is impressive and little changed, at least, until the eyes are lowered, for the modern town is, of course, very much larger, but the horizon must be exactly the same. I find it harder to share Mrs Radcliffe's sentiments, however, having donated my bowler hat to the moths, but then I am more used to horrors than even Mrs Radcliffe hearing almost daily from Ulster of how the revolution turned out to be not so 'glorious' after all.

On the other side of the river on Castle Hill there is a less explicit but more revered monument. It was on this oval-shaped mound that the Normans developed a stout stone castle as garrison for the Barony of Kendal. Situated some six hundred yards from the church the castle had an excellent view to the north and south-west. As we have seen, this Norman building was by no means the first to occupy the site, but it was by far the most secure and, as the bastion of the barony, was of great importance. It is strange, therefore, that so little is known of the castle's early history. If it is compared with other Westmorland castles, Brough or Appleby, say, or even Pendragon in the Mallerstang Valley, almost nothing is known about it. It is true those on the Eden achieved a kind of false notoriety because they were each so carefully restored by Lady Anne Clifford towards the end of the seventeenth century, though her exertions achieved little except in the case of Appleby which became the home of her descendants. Kendal lacked even an enthusiast. Camden, writing at the beginning of the seventeenth century, describes a castle 'ready to drop down with age', a fact of which the owners must have been well aware. When some years before, in 1572, a survey was prepared for the Marchioness of Northampton, only the dovecote was listed as being in good repair. The castle, however, had 'walls, circular, guarded by three towers, and a keep, with a large square area in the centre, being all in a state of dilapidation'.

What can we say of the castle in its heyday? Precious little. It was probably begun during the time of the first Lord of Kendal, Ivo de Tailbois, but a castle of such a size would take a long time to complete, if it is possible to speak of 'completion' in the case of a building which was in all likelihood altered and strengthened by succeeding owners. Much work is thought to have been carried out in the twelfth century during the time of Gilbert Fitz-Reinfred, so that by the thirteenth century there was a large complex of buildings on the site. The material used was principally the dark grey Silurian rock of the hills east of Kendal. This was tougher than the Kendal limestone. The doors and windows were jambed in red sandstone as were the quoins in most instances, and dressed stones were placed at the angles of buildings, though Kendal probably needed fewer than many castles of the period since most of the towers were circular and the main curtain wall ran round in the oval shape of the hill on which it was built.

The main gatehouse was on the north side and it seems the main approach to the castle was from the north, that is, from the Stramongate end of the town. There is nothing of the gatehouse left for us to see, but we may assume it would have had a portcullis and a drawbridge. There may be something to be believed in a small drawing, now in the museum, said to be a copy of one drawn in Sir Thomas Parr's time that showed the gatehouse with two towers of unequal height, but there is no definite evidence to go on. What we can see from the ruins gives us an idea of the size of the place: many of the walls are five feet thick or wider; there were altogether five towers of various sizes, and, though mostly round, there seems to have been one square tower on the south side. The Great Hall, probably the main living quarters, was on the north-east side where today only little stubs of wall and two barrel-vaulted cellars of unequal height remain. It is likely to have been in one of the rooms in this part of the castle that Katherine Parr was born, but more of her later.

Ivo de Tailbois and the Kendal Barons

In most early histories of the County of Westmorland Ivo de Tailbois is given as the first Lord, or Baron, of Kendal, which is undoubtedly true; but then we are told that the Kendal lands had been granted by William the Conqueror as a reward for de Tailbois' part in the Norman invasion, which is false. It was, in fact, William Rufus who rewarded de Tailbois for supporting his claim to the English throne rather than that of his brother, the Conqueror's eldest son, Robert. This grant of land was made right at the beginning of the reign before William marched north to take Carlisle in 1092. De Tailbois was already a considerable landowner having inherited through his wife, Lucia, the Manor of Spalding in Lincolnshire, and most of what was known as Holland in that region. Lucia was the daughter of Thorold, the English Lord of Spalding, and she had married de Tailbois some time prior to the year 1074. With this new grant of land in the North de Tailbois became the holder of the vast area known as Amounderness, made up of dozens of manors, which the Conqueror had formerly granted to Roger de Poitou, but which were forfeited when de Poitou supported a rebellion against the Crown. Amounderness included all Lancashire north of the River Ribble; Ewecross in Yorkshire; much of south-west Cumberland; and the land of the Barony of Kendal, though it must be remembered that names like Lancashire and Cumberland were not used at that time. As he seems so important, who was this Ivo de Tailbois?

To begin with, de Tailbois was never a Norman but an Angevin, that is, he came from Anjou, a county, in the true sense, situated south of Normandy, the land of the future Plantagenets. The name de Tailbois, the 'Woodchopper', almost certainly began as a nickname, and I suspect this 'chopper' was better with heads than with wood, for the Normans had many such Angevin fighters among their ranks, and de Tailbois, renowned for his tough physique, courage and tactical ability, was good at fighting. He was given the task of 'removing' the rebel, Hereward the Wake, from the Isle of Ely, territory in which he as Lord of Spalding and Holland had an interest. In Charles Kingsley's novel *Hereward the Wake*, de Tailbois is characterized as the most typical of the ruthless, usurping Norman conquerors. Yet, there is little doubt about de Tailbois' generosity to the Church. As Lord of Spalding he granted a small Saxon monastery that had been founded in 1052 to the large Abbey of St Nicholas at Angiers, an arrangement that was not very successful. But that cannot be said of his gift to the new Abbey of St Mary, York. St Mary's had been founded in 1088, and the earliest existing record concerning Kendal states that 'Ivo de Tailbois gave to St Mary's, York, the church of Kircabi in Kendale with its land.' In fact, de Tailbois' generosity to St Mary's knew no bounds, and he granted it several churches including ones at Kirkby Stephen and Kirkby Lonsdale.

It is thought that de Tailbois may have been a member of the royal house of Anjou, a brother of the Count, but there is no evidence one way or the other, and it is just as likely, as one scholar argues, that like William the Conqueror himself, he was illegitimate.

It is not known when Ivo de Tailbois died, nor is it known with any certainty who succeeded him, though the names Eltred or Ethelred, and Ketel are usually given as the second and third Barons of Kendal for lack of further evidence, and it is assumed that they were members of the de Tailbois family. Gilbert, son of Ketel, is usually considered the fourth Baron of Kendal, and he was succeeded by his son, William de Tailbois. It was this William de Tailbois who changed the family name to de Lancaster because he was, among other things, Governor of Lancaster Castle, which was more important than Kendal. Things might have been very different had he called himself William de Kendal!

Very little is known about de Lancaster except for his interest in several religious houses, including Furness and Cockersand Abbeys, St Bees, and, as we have seen already, the Leper Hospital of St Leonard's, near Kendal. He is also thought to have been the founder of Conishead Priory. However, by far the most significant fact from our point of view was his decision to live at Lancaster, in the fine castle built by Roger de Poitou, and not at Kendal, though it may be assumed he visited Kendal from time to time and made sure the place was in good repair.

William de Lancaster had married Gundred, the daughter of the Earl Warrenne, and he was succeeded by their son, another William, which leads to confusions, particularly as there is a third William de Lancaster to come! In order to make things easier, the three Williams are usually given numbers which is the simplest way of dealing with the problem. William de Lancaster II, then, reached a position of importance in the Court of Henry II, and he was appointed Steward. He married Helwise Stutville and they produced a daughter, their only child, who was named after her mother. The younger Helwise married the son of Roger Fitz-Reinfred, Gilbert, which is how Gilbert Fitz-Reinfred comes into the picture. Although he only gained the title by marriage, Gilbert Fitz-Reinfred became the sixth Baron of Kendal, and it is likely that he did live at Kendal Castle. Fitz-Reinfred was granted many privileges by King Richard I, including the weekly Saturday market in Kendal. He was one of the barons who forced King John to sign the Magna Carta in 1215.

In 1219, Gilbert died to be succeeded by his son, William Fitz-Reinfred, who decided to revert to his mother's family name calling himself William de Lancaster after his grandfather. We shall refer to him as William de Lancaster III. He became very important in the history of Kendal for the simple fact that he had no children by his wife, Agnes de Brus, thus causing the barony to be divided up between his two sisters, another Helwise, and Alice. Perhaps we should refer to Helwise III!

The Marquis, Lumley and Richmond Fees
When reading about the Kendal area I constantly came across three phrases: the Richmond Fee, the Marquis Fee and the Lumley Fee, and I wondered what on earth they meant. It turned out to be fairly simple once I had sorted it all out, but having done so it may be of help to others if I make my account as simple as possible.

William de Lancaster III, then, was the last of the Kendal barons to possess the whole estate, and having no children to inherit, the barony was divided more or less equally between

Helwise and Alice Fitz-Reinfred, who were both married. Let us consider Helwise first.

Helwise had married a cousin of her mother's called Peter de Brus, sometimes spelt Bruce, and produced five children, four girls: Margaret, Agnes, Lucy and Laderina; and a boy: Peter, named after his father. Now, had Peter lived to father children the whole story would have been different, but he died unmarried in 1278, and so his estate was divided between his four sisters. Margaret, the eldest, had married Robert de Roos; she inherited Kendal Castle, three-quarters of the town, and land to the north and west 'in demesnes, villages, rents, and service of free men and others except the village of Kentmere'. Margaret de Roos was a widow at the time, her husband having died in 1273, but they had produced children, and it is through the de Rooses that the Parr family comes into the Kendal story.

Margaret's great-great-grandson, John de Roos, had an only daughter who married William Parr. This Parr line continued through many generations until in 1547 William Parr, Queen Katherine's brother, was created Marquis of Northampton by Henry VIII, so that the land he held in the Kendal Barony became known as the Marquis Fee, a fee being the term for a feudal benefice.

Fortunately, Agnes, the second sister of Peter de Brus, gives us no problem, for although she did inherit a large estate it was made up of land outside Westmorland. What of Lucy, the third sister? Lucy had married a gentleman with the splendid name of Marmaduke de Thweng and her share of the estate was mostly the land west of the town, though she held a quarter of the town itself. For years the de Thwengs remained in possession of the Lyth Valley as far north as Grasmere, until a later member of the family was called to the priesthood becoming the Priest-in-Charge of Beetham. This priest, Thomas de Thweng, left his estate to one of his sisters, another Lucy, who had married into the Lumley Family, and to another Marmaduke! Ah, so this is the Lumley Fee:

It will be remembered that Kentmere was excluded from the estate Margaret de Roos inherited. This was because it was the only part that came to the youngest sister, Laderina. As the youngest Laderina's share was the smallest, but Kentmere was not to be sneezed at. Laderina had married a Yorkshire gentleman, John de Bella-Aqua, and it was through her eldest daughter, Sibilla, who married into the Stapleton Family, that Kentmere remained in the Stapleton's hands until the reign of Charles I.

I have left the Richmond Fee until the last because it is slightly more complicated, but I intend to simplify it. To begin with, William de Lancaster III left his estate to his two sisters, Helwise and Alice. Alice, the younger sister, married into the de Lyndesay family and by her husband, William de Lyndesay, had a son, Walter, who inherited her estate. This Walter de Lyndesay's grandson died leaving an only daughter, Christian, who had married a Frenchman, de Coucy, which made things very complicated, for the Lords de Coucy, being aliens, could not inherit the estate and it reverted to the Crown. That might have been the end of the de Coucy involvement, but one of them married the daughter of Edward III, and held the property, passing it on through the line until again through lack of children it reverted to the Crown.

From this last reversion the estate was held by various people including John, Duke of Bedford, during the reign of Henry VI. It was Henry VII who granted it to his mother, Margaret, Countess of Richmond, and it was through her holding of the estate that it became known as the Richmond Fee, and not, as was once thought, through Henry VIII's natural son, the Duke of Richmond who also held it. From this time onwards the Richmond Fee was held by the Crown, and handed out at will. Charles II, for instance, granted it to his wife, Catherine of Braganza, from which time the estate was often referred to as the Queen's Lands. Some have thought that this last title has something to do with Queen Katherine Parr, but, as we have seen, the Parr family were the holders of the Marquis Fee. It seems our 'fees' are now all paid, but never Kendal's debt to the Parrs.

Katherine Parr, Queen of England

Katherine Parr may have been Queen of England, but she has been Queen of Kendal ever since. There are roads named after her. She has a cocktail bar in the County Hotel, and hundreds of Kendal children 'creep unwillingly' or eagerly, as the case may be, into Queen Katherine's School! Nobody comes up to her achievement: a girl born just outside the town on a little hill to the east who was destined to become the sixth of the King's six wives. Katherine, whom Winston Churchill described as 'a serious little widow from the Lake District, learned, and interested in theological questions' married her king at Hampton Court on July, 1542. It sounds good enough, but what really happened?

In marrying Henry VIII Katherine was doing what she was told. She was forced to obey, even before she promised to obey. She had tried her best to evade the proposal; 'Sire, it were better to be your mistress than your wife,' she is reported to have said. Better by far, for as a mistress she would not have been required to give very much, since by 1542 Henry was a wreck and impotent. He had suppurating ulcers on his legs which became worse with the mercury treatment he was receiving for their cure; he was so gross that a system of pullies had to be erected to move him about the palace; he was maudlin and bad-tempered, and in his cups was given to bouts of uncontrolled weeping. Disgusting would not be too strong a word for a man who had divorced two and murdered two other wives, and yet this good-natured woman, twice herself widowed, one might even say this holy woman, Katherine, gave herself to him, not that he was capable of consummating the gift. Why did she do it? She dared not refuse. She had wished to marry an equally worthless man, Thomas Seymour, though he was attractive and not as scheming as the King. The King, seeing this love, for Katherine was in love, intervened, just as he had done in the case of his fifth wife, Catherine Howard, who on the scaffold had lamented: 'I die a Queen, but would rather die the wife of Culpeper.' Katherine Parr only just escaped a similar fate, but there is little doubt that the marriage was a success, and for the King's unfortunate children Katherine was a godsend. For Prince Edward and Princess Elizabeth Katherine was the only 'mother' they had known. Who, then, was this remarkable Kendal woman known as the 'one who outlived him', and almost the 'one who got away'?

Katherine Parr was born in 1512, probably at Kendal Castle, though it is by no means certain, for her father, Sir Thomas Parr, was Master of the Wards and Comptroller of the King's Household, and would have had a London residence. Katherine's mother, Maud Green, was the daughter of Sir Thomas Green, of Broughton and Green's Norton in Northamptonshire, and she had married Thomas Parr when she was barely 13 years old, in 1508. She may have been just 18 when her first child, Katherine, was born, though there were to be two others, William and Anne.

It should not worry the Kendal folk that there is some doubt that Katherine was born at the castle, because there is no doubt whatsoever that when Sir Thomas died in 1517 Lady Parr brought her three young children to Kendal, and that Katherine spent her childhood there. Lady Parr was only 22 years old at the time, and refusing several offers of marriage devoted her life to her children. She employed the best tutors and governesses, so that during the early years of her life at Kendal Katherine, who was an exceptionally bright child, obtained a fluency in Latin, Greek and French, and a working knowledge of Italian. By all accounts she was alert and somewhat precocious: she is reputed to have retorted to her mother's stricture that she should apply herself more earnestly to her spinning and weaving, in which she was a true Kendalian, 'My hands are ordained to touch crowns and sceptres, and not spindles and needles.' In this reply, it seems, Katherine was elaborating upon certain astrological predictions that 'she was born to sit on the highest seat of imperial majesty'.

In 1523, when Katherine was barely twelve, she was married to Edward, Lord Borough, of Gainsborough in Lincolnshire, an exceptionally old man in his dotage, said to have been 'distracted in memory'. Such extraordinary matches were quite common at the time, and, of course, they were 'arranged', the pros and cons being weighed up on the matters of breeding and money. The protagonists of any match were regarded much in the way dogs and racehorses are today. Lady Parr had, for instance, refused Lord Scrope's son for Katherine when the idea was mooted by Lord Dacre. Dacre had written to Scrope to the effect that 'unless he married his son to an heiress of land he did not think he could marry him to so good stock as Lady Parr's considering her wisdom and the wise stock of the Greens whence she is come, and of the Parrs of Kendal'. Apart from the term 'stock' which keeps recurring in such advice, it is interesting to note that Katherine was not an 'heiress of land', which was true while her brother, William, lived. However, when old Lord Borough died in 1529, after six years of marriage, Katherine was left a rich widow with estates in Lincolnshire, Yorkshire and Nottinghamshire. What did she do with all her riches? She returned home to Kendal.

Katherine was probably at the castle when her mother died in 1529 but, it seems, she soon moved to Sizergh Castle where her step-son, Henry Borough, was living with his wife, Katherine Neville, Lady Strickland. It was at Sizergh that Katherine was to meet her second husband, John Neville, Lord Latimer, of Snape Hall in Yorkshire. He had been twice widowed, his first wife having been another local woman, Elizabeth Musgrave, from Edenhall. Latimer had extensive estates which he settled on Katherine, who took on the role of mother to his two children, John and Margaret Neville, whose studies she supervised much in the way her own mother had done, and she too availed herself of the children's tutors. While she was married to Latimer Katherine became involved in public events for the first time when her husband sided with the rebels in the Pilgrimage of Grace in 1536, and became one of the delegates to bargain with the Duke of Norfolk, the King's representative. Luckily for Latimer, he took no part in the second phase of the rebellion. This may have been through Katherine's advice, for she herself was able to persuade the King, in 1540, to release Sir George Throgmorton, her aunt's husband, from prison. Throgmorton had been accused of treason on false evidence drummed up by Thomas Cromwell, and it has been said that Katherine's interview with the King not only introduced Henry to his future wife but brought about Cromwell's downfall. In 1542, Lord Latimer died, leaving Katherine a widow once more.

Almost immediately Katherine was in demand as a wife; this time by Sir Thomas Seymour, the brother of Queen Jane Seymour who had died in childbirth giving Henry his long-awaited male heir, in 1537. It is thought that Seymour took a lease on Helsington Laithes so as to be close to Sizergh where Katherine was again living. Katherine, as I have said, was attracted by Seymour, and there is no doubt that his proposal would have been accepted had not the King intervened. The royal marriage took place in the July of 1543; both the princesses, Mary and Elizabeth, were present, and the Bishop of

Winchester, Stephen Gardiner, presided, which, in view of what
would happen later, was ironic.

The degree of Henry's trust in his new wife is shown by the Act
passed in 1544 to ensure that any children born to Katherine
should have the right of succession after Prince Edward, though
the possibility of children was slight. Also, Henry made Katherine Regent during his absence when he crossed over the Channel to take part in the French War, his part being to be carried
about in a litter! Katherine was not even crowned Queen, but
several specimens of her signature have survived from her
Regency; they are signed 'Kateryn, the Queen Regent, K.P.'.
The 'K.P.' stands for her maiden name, Katherine Parr, which
proves that she herself spelt her name with a K, as we might
expect a good Kendal girl to do, but I notice that many eminent
scholars have adopted a C in their ignorance!

As Regent Katherine ordered a public thanksgiving for the
capture of Boulogne on the 19th of September, 1544, the port
that Henry was to refer to as 'his daughter', and he was more
concerned about that 'daughter' than either of the two girls
whose welfare was now left to Katherine to administer. It is
thought that it was through her encouragement that the Princess Mary translated Erasmus's *Paraphrases* on the New Testa-
ment, and Elizabeth *The Mirror of Glass of the Sinful Soul*.
Katherine's care for the children took up much of her time,
though she organized intimate prayer meetings for her ladies-
in-waiting at which the Bible was read and discussed. She
herself had published in 1545 *The Prayers stirring the Mind
unto Heavenly Meditations*. There is little doubt but that
Katherine was very much more in sympathy with Protestant-
ism than her husband, a fact that disturbed the mind of Bishop
Gardiner, who with Wriothesley, the Chancellor, drew up articles of heresy against her which the King signed. Katherine
came to learn of the peril she was in, it is said, because Wriothesley accidentally dropped the document in the corridor of the
Palace of Whitehall, and its contents were conveyed to the
Queen by her doctor. Katherine avoided arrest and trial, and
almost certain execution, by flattery. In this she was magnificent. She is reported to have told the King: 'God hath appointed
you as the supreme head of us all, and of you, next unto God, will
I ever learn.' This was music to the King's ears, for he was

always haunted by the memory that some of his closest friends, men like Sir Thomas More and Bishop Fisher, had gone to their deaths rather than accept the King's supremacy. The conversation between the King and Katherine is worth noting, for it reveals how subtle her handling of him was:

'Not so, by St Mary, you are become a Doctor, Kate, to instruct us, and not to be instructed of us, as oft-times we have seen.'

'Indeed, if your Majesty have so conceived, my meaning has been mistaken, for I have always held it preposterous for a woman to instruct her lord; and if I have ever presumed to differ with your Highness on religion, it was partly to obtain information for my own comfort, regarding certain nice points on which I stood in doubt, and sometimes because I perceived that, in talking, you were better able to pass away the pain and weariness of your present infirmity, which encouraged me to this boldness, in the hope of profiting by your Majesty's learned discourse.'

After such brilliant subterfuge how could Henry but reply: 'And be it so, sweetheart? Then we are perfect friends.' Whatever else it did, this approach saved Katherine's life, for when Gardiner and Wriothesley arrived at Hampton Court with a platoon of pikemen to arrest the Queen, the King told them to 'avaunt from his presence'.

Henry VIII died at the end of the January of 1547. In his will he noted 'the great love, obedience, chastity of life, and wisdom being in our fore-named wife and queen', and he left Katherine three thousand pounds in plate, jewels, and household goods, 'and such apparel as it shall please her to take', together with a thousand pounds in money.

Katherine moved to Chelsea Palace, and it was there that Sir Thomas Seymour, only thirty-four days after the King's death, exchanged marriage contracts and rings, though the actual wedding ceremony took place about a month later. The couple moved to Sudeley, but Seymour proved to be an unfaithful husband, and Katherine's suffering in this was increased when she realized that the chief object of her husband's affections was the 15-year-old Princess Elizabeth of whom Katherine was guardian. On one occasion, although she herself was pregnant, Katherine caught her husband with Elizabeth in his arms. All this meant that Katherine's first pregnancy was fraught with anxiety, though she never blamed Elizabeth for a moment. Seymour, who was now Lord Admiral, was often away during this time. The episode with Elizabeth had taken place during the Whit week of 1548, Whit Sunday falling that year on the 20th of May. On the 30th of August Katherine gave birth to a baby daughter, but puerperal fever set in and, having refused the attention of her own doctor, she died on the 7th of September; the child, Mary, survived. Katherine was 36 when she ended her holy and unhappy life, and she must, surely, have looked upon those early days in Kendal as the best. In the little silver-bound prayer book, today kept safe in the Mayor's Parlour in Kendal, she wrote: 'How often have I been disappointed where I thought I should have found friendship: and how often have I found it where I least thought, therefore it is a vain thing to trust in man, for the true trust and health of man is only in Thee. Blessed be Thou, Lord, therefore in all things that happen to us: for we are weak and unstable, soon deceived and soon changed from one thing to another.'

Katherine's funeral was held from Sudeley Castle, the home she had known for those last months of her life, and she was buried inside the church at Sudeley. The chief mourner was a young girl, just ten years old, who would soon enter on to the sad stage of Tudor affairs. Her name was Lady Jane Grey.

William Parr, Marquis of Northampton

Among the mourners at Katherine Parr's funeral was her younger brother, William, whose life has been eclipsed by the fame of his sister. William had been born in 1515, and must have been only 4 when he came into the Kendal estate, though this was managed by his mother until her death. William had benefited from the careful education his mother had provided at the castle, and all his life he maintained the love of music and poetry fostered during those Kendal days. William Parr was a man whom people respected: Henry VIII referred to him as 'his integrity', and the young Prince Edward used to speak of his 'honest uncle', presumably in contrast to his Seymour uncles.

In 1539, Henry VIII created William Lord Parr and Roos, of Kendal, and later, at about the time of the royal marriage in 1543, Baron of Hart, in Northamptonshire, although already through his first marriage to Lady Anne Bouchier, the only

Highgate, Kendal
Stramongate Bridge, Kendal

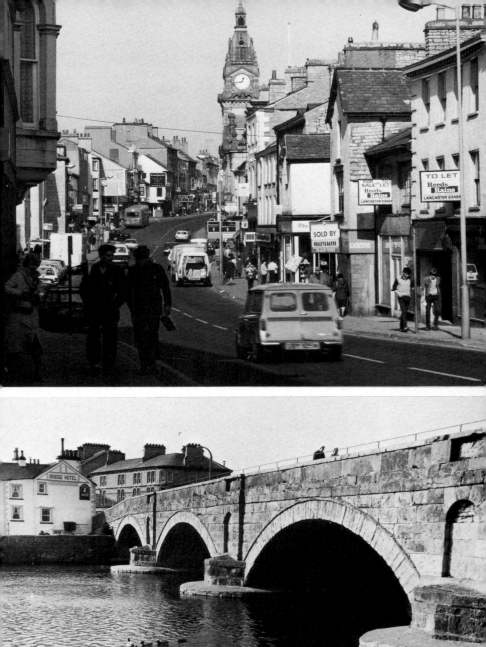

daughter and heir of the Earl of Essex, he was honoured with the courtesy title of the Earl of Essex on the death of his father-in-law.

During the first weeks of Edward VI's reign a further title of the Marquis of Northampton was conferred upon William, thus, as shown, bringing the term Marquis Fee into our history. At this time it seemed as though more honours might be given, but it was not to be so, for when King Edward died and Queen Mary succeeded to the throne William Parr was one of those who supported the claim of Lady Jane Grey. A charge of treason was brought against him and, as with the Earl of Northumberland, his estates were forfeited together with all his titles. It seems that he only just escaped the fate of Northumberland who was executed, but possibly Queen Mary found it too hard to condemn one to death who was not the instigator of the affair and the brother of Katherine whom she had loved. Two years later, in 1556, the Queen decided to give William back his estates, or part of them, 'all those demesne lands without the walls of the said park of Kendal, and the mill and burgages in the village or burgh of the Manor of Kendal.' However, his titles were not restored to him until the reign of Queen Elizabeth, when for 'favouring the Protestant religion' all his former titles and honours were given back.

William Parr was to be married three times. The first marriage was annulled because of Lady Anne's adultery in 1551. Next he married Elizabeth Brook, the daughter of Lord Cobham, and after her death he married a Swedish girl called Helena Suavendurg, who, according to Bishop Parkhurst of Norwich, was 'very beautiful'. We have to take the Bishop's word for it.

William lived until he was 56 and he died in 1571 to be buried with rosemary and bay leaves in his coffin in the choir of the large collegiate church in Warwick. 'A sincere, plain, direct man; not crafty nor involved.'

Kirkland

It is time now to leave the castle and its history and cross over the River Kent to the small township of Kirkland which was once separated from the Borough of Kendal by the small beck, aptly named from the Old Norse word meaning 'hidden', Blind

The New Shambles, Kendal

Beck. Once houses were constructed about it the beck would become so familiar as to be hardly noticed, though the name seems to have been derived from the 'hidden' aspects of its source on the limestone rocks of Gilling Grove. Blind Beck formed the northern boundary of Kirkland, and today it runs behind houses, beneath the road, and beside Abbot Hall with, in the summer, 'roses, roses, all the way', until it reaches the Kent just as it has always done. A little to the south of it the Angles built their little church, and one may take it that there was some kind of a settlement already in existence when they arrived. The native folk often developed small settlements just outside the confines of military outposts, many taking over those positions after the Romans left, as I have suggested. It is thought there may have been such a settlement by Castle Howe on Beast Banks, but there is no evidence besides probability. On the other hand it is certain that a settlement did develop at Kirkland across the river from Castle Hill, the old Roman position on which a Roman coin was unearthed fairly recently.

The Kirk

The Angles built a church, though perhaps I should explain that for architectural purposes all building of the period is known as Saxon, although the real Saxons never came anywhere near Kendal. This is why there are many references in old directories to a 'Saxon' church. Nothing, however, is known of the design or dimensions of the early church, and all that remains to persuade us that there was a church of Kendal in those days is a fragment of an Anglian cross, a smaller fragment than the fine example to be seen at Heversham; and the name of the place itself, Kirkby, though that is Norse and not Anglian:

The church which stands today on the same site as the earlier building reminds me of the great 'wool' churches of East Anglia, and, of course, wool was largely responsible for the prosperous 'look' of Kendal Parish Church, for as the wool trade boomed so the church was enlarged and beautified to meet the needs of an expanding congregation. The building is 140 feet long and 103 feet wide, which makes it only a fraction narrower than the parish church at Great Yarmouth, the widest church in the country. The roof at Kendal is held up by thirty-two pillars. The oldest parts of the building are the chancel and nave, both of the thirteenth century but much restored. There is evidence that the Scots led by the Earl of Fife entered Kendal in 1210 and burnt and pillaged the town, ransacking the church and killing at random anyone in sight. It is said that many seeking sanctuary in the churchyard were cut down and of these many were women and children. Rightly has that day been recorded as 'Kendal's saddest day'. After this raid the church was in need of repair, but it seems that it was not until 1232 that much of the work was carried out. In that year an indulgence was issued for essential repairs to Kendal Church, then in a desperate state of ruin. The same kind of money-raising was provided in the middle of the fifteenth century, and it is a sign of how the people valued their church. The west tower was probably added at this time, while the clerestory, the aisles, both inner and outer, and chapels were added a little later. The north chapel is known as the Bellingham Chapel because it was donated before his death by Sir Roger Bellingham, in 1553. The south chapel, known as the Parr Chapel, is probably a little earlier than this. However, there are two further chapels named after important families, the Strickland Chapel at the west end of the inner south aisle, and what is known as the Chambre Chapel at the east end of the inner north aisle. Many members of these families are buried inside the church, particularly Sir Roger Bellingham, and Sir William Parr who was the grandfather of Queen Katherine.

There are many interesting tablets and brasses to be seen. One odd and amusing brass is to Rev. Ralph Tirer who was Vicar of Kendal from 1592 to 1627, and who is reported to have written the inscription himself. It reads:

> London bredd me, Westminster fed me,
> Cambridge sped me, my Sister wed me.
> Study taught me, Living sought me,
> Learning brought me, Kendal caught me,
> Labour pressed me, sickness distressed me,
> Death oppressed me, & grave possessed me,
> God first gave me, Christ did save me,
> Earth did crave me, and would have me.

Surely if the good Vicar really had married his sister it is most unlikely that heaven would have taken him at all.

There are also monuments to Zachery Hubbersty, George Romney and George Sedgwick, who was secretary to Lady Anne Clifford, while somewhere by the Strickland Chapel Father Thomas West is said to be buried. West was the author of *The Antiquities of Furness* and *Guide to the Lakes*, which was the first of the long list of guides that have appeared since. It came out in 1778, so if you find too unruly a crowd up on Striding Edge you can always blame him, for Wordsworth was only 8 years old when West's book was published.

Thomas West who had been born in Inverness in 1720, later entered the Society of Jesus and joined the Jesuit Mission in Furness, which centred on Bardsea Manor owned by the Preston family. As Father West, however, he lived at Titeup Hall, near Dalton, having arrived there in 1766, 'my principal comfort to be of some service to a few people' he wrote. It was while he was at Titeup Hall that he began work on *The Antiquities of Furness, or An Account of the Royal Abbey of St Mary*, published in London in 1774, and four years later *A Guide to the Lakes*, 'dedicated to the lovers of the landscape studies and to all who have visited or intend to visit the Lakes in Cumberland, Westmorland and Lancashire'. The book appeared in the same year as the First Catholic Relief Act was passed which was to bring the Penal Days to an end. He died on the 10th of July, 1779, at the age of 62, and was buried in Kendal Church according to his own wish.

The church at Kendal had been granted to St Mary's Abbey at York by the first Lord of Kendal, Ivo de Tailbois, as we have seen, and William de Lancaster later allowed the abbey a grant of land, so that the abbey's interests became quite considerable in the Kirkland. The Benedictine abbey at York had been founded during the reign of William II in 1088. The first Abbot, Stephen, who had been Prior of Whitby and Lastingham Abbeys, was consecrated by Thomas of Bayeux, Archbishop of York. St Mary's was one of the most important abbeys in the country, and its abbot, as a Peer of Parliament, even had a London house. He also had a house in Kendal. What is now known as Abbot Hall, the Kendal Art Gallery, is a house built by George Wilson, the fourth son of Daniel Wilson of Dallam Tower, on old abbey lands, perhaps on the site of the earlier Abbot's dwelling. The history of Abbot Hall since its beginning in 1759 to its happy present state makes pretty boring reading for it seems that owning Abbot Hall was, during the nineteenth century anyway, a status symbol and several usurers muscled in until it was bought by the Kendal Corporation for £3,750, a sum about a thousand pounds cheaper than the place had changed hands for in 1772. This final purchase was made possible largely through the generous contribution of the Kendal Savings Bank, which put up £2,500 on condition that most of the grounds would be made into a public park. The house after some deliberation was made into an art gallery and cultural centre. The gallery part I understand, but the Centre sounds too much like a health and sports centre for my liking. However, on 28th September 1962, Princess Margaret and Lord Snowdon came to Kendal to open the gallery.

This venture might have been local, but without backing from the Provincial Insurance Company it might have been impossible. It has developed largely because of the determination, energy and sheer daring of the present Director, Mary Burkett. In her, Kendal has been most fortunate, for it is her vision that has made what one sees today possible. Abbot Hall has many treasures: there are paintings by Reynolds, Turner and Romney, besides several other portraits by Daniel Gardner, another artist who began his career in Kendal; furniture by Chippendale Sheraton, and from nearer home, several pieces by Gillow of Lancaster; there is a Clementi piano; and an embroidered map of 1792 worked by M. Dearman is in the hall where there is also a fine tall clock made by a Kirkby Lonsdale clockmaker, Peter Hathornethwaite.

Of the Romneys three are worth mention: two of these are rather similar full-length portraits, which are fairly early works dating from about 1760. In one, Captain Banks, dressed in blue and with the fist of his left hand clenched into his waist, stands against a seascape. In his right hand he holds a book rested lightly upon a rock. The portrait of John Postlethwaite is very much more relaxed. Though the pose is similar as is Postlethwaite's dress, a very light-brown frock-coat, waistcoat and breeches with white stockings, he leans almost nonchalantly on a plinth. His right hand is tucked away which will have saved Romney a little time in the painting, and is fortunate anyway, since the hand he has painted looks like plaster.

The contrast between the two early portraits and the magnificent painting of the Gower family which graces the dining-room could hardly be more marked. Here one sees Romney at his very best. Quite apart from the appealing theme of four young children dancing round in a ring while an older child bangs a tambourine, Romney has managed to goad the little quartet into motion so that one almost begins to feel dizzy gazing at the dance. I know little or nothing about the tricks employed, but I suspect that by giving the older girl with the tambourine a rather stiff classical pose, so that one can hardly believe that she is really banging the instrument at all, the children appear to swing round so that the child on the right, who seems to be leading the dance, almost swings out of the canvas on to the museum floor. It is exceptional for a small gallery to have a painting of such importance and Kendal should be exceedingly proud. Everyone should go to see it as often as possible. The painting arrived in Kendal with considerable help from outside; gifts came from the Victoria and Albert Museum Grant-in-Aid Fund, the Government, Westmorland County Council, the National Art-Collections Fund, The Provincial Insurance Company, and many other smaller grants from individuals. One can only say thank God and well done. The best of Romney has come home.

Across the courtyard of the main house the stable block has been converted into a Museum of Lakeland Life and Industry. This was opened in 1971 by Princess Alexandra, and there is much to see of local interest, tools of various crafts, a bobbin-turning machine and a threshing machine, displays of mining, quarrying, weaving and spinning. I think I enjoy most the room furnished and decorated as a Westmorland farmhouse bedroom. I could sleep comfortably and peacefully there.

Kendal Grammar School

Also situated in the vicinity of Abbot Hall is the old grammar school building. The school was housed there from 1588 until 1889 when a new building was opened in the Lound.

Kendal Grammar School had been founded in 1525, some years before the first building was provided and the same year, as it happens, that Roger Lupton founded a school at Sedbergh. The boys would have been taught in the church to begin with, and it was to provide a suitable priest to act as schoolmaster of this free school in Kendal that Adam Penyngton, a gentleman from Boston in Lincolnshire, left £10 in his will. The endowment was to come from lands held by the Penyngtons in Lincolnshire and it was to last for a period of ninety-eight years. However, the Penyngton property reverted to the Crown, so that, in 1548, Edward VI's Commissioners 'ordained that the Grammar School which long before had been kept in Kirkby Kendal should be continued there, assuring the master there to have his wages yearly, the said £10.' After this happy confirmation from the Crown Commissioners of Edward VI, it seems that by the time Elizabeth was on the throne various irregularities had set in. By 1557 the Kendal schoolmaster complained that his stipend had been withheld, a matter which the Law had to sort out. Land was needed for a building, and this was provided by Miles Philipson, of Crook, who donated a portion of the grounds of Abbot Hall. The school building was paid for largely by public subscription, but the Earl Ambrose and the Countess of Warwick gave six oak trees for the main timbers while local folk were expected to supply floor timbers and stone.

The school flourished during the seventeenth and eighteenth centuries sending many boys on to the universities, though by the middle of the nineteenth century it seems to have gone into a decline so that it was decided to amalgamate the grammar school with the Blue Coat School which I shall consider later. A board of governors was appointed to be known as 'The Governors of the United School and Hospital Foundation of Kendal'. New premises were found and opened in 1889, and four years later a headmaster's house was added with sufficient room for about forty boarders. These premises are still in use and, indeed, an amalgamation of schools has occurred again quite recently when Kendal Grammar School for Boys joined with Kendal High School for Girls. What a merry get-together that has been, and the school now keeps alive the old name of the town, for it is called Kirkby Kendal School.

The Kirkland Anchorite
On Speed's map of Kendal issued in 1614 there is an anchorage marked, or, as Speed spells it, an ankeriche. There is still an Anchorite Road and Anchorite Fields by Kirkbarrow, the 'hill

above the church', and the tradition is very early that an anchorite, that is a hermit or recluse, a holy man anyway, settled beside a well in a small beehive hut in about 1176. The earliest record I have discovered is one of 1430 which speaks of 'an anchorite's house built next to the church in Kirkby in Kendal', though the original is in Latin. Various legends as to the hermit's reasons for taking up such an austere life have grown around this simple fact of there being an anchorage in Kendal. Here is one which is related by John F. Curwen in his book *Kirkbie-Kendall*:

It was towards the end of the reign of King Edward III that an Anchorite appeared in Kendal in the habit of a palmer, with the crossed staff, the robe, and the broad flat hat decorated with a cockle shell upon his tanned and withered forehead, which denoted that he had been to the Holy Land. Nobody enquired who or what the pilgrim was, for the class were as common as commercial travellers are today; but, although he lived on the humblest fare, he bestowed much money in alms on the lepers and licensed beggars who infested the highways, sat before the cross houses, or hung around the church doorways. After a time he busied himself in collecting stones from the fell-side, and having purchased a small piece of land from the Abbey of St Mary's at York, he constructed for himself a hovel, furnished with the rudest and simplest materials, and took up his abode by this spring. But gossip and curiosity soon began to be aroused concerning the stranger, who had laid aside his staff and changed his pilgrim's weeds to assume a course white cassock of Kendal cloth, and who was always busy cultivating the ground attached to his cell by the well side. The Anchorite was deemed a holy man, and the spring became the resort of the afflicted, who fondly thought that its pure waters and the prayers of the hermit, versed in the healing arts of the East, were capable of performing miracles. At last he fell sick unto death, and confessed to Father Ralf the story of his only love. Long years gone by, his Blanche was all to him, smiling upon and sharing his every dream of happiness, embroidered his scarf, and wrought the blazon of his knightly pennon when he won his spurs by capturing a Scottish chief. They never spoke of love; theirs was no lip worship. The two souls intermingled, as it were, by instinct, and both were blessed; until one day, whilst staying at Kendal Castle, an usurping brother's love marred all His Blanche was lost to him, fear succeeded to frenzy, and that same night he concealed their bodies beside this well. Selling his

The Lyth Valley from Scout Scar
The old Sedbergh road

patrimony he assumed the cross, hoping to lose his burden by warfare against the infidels; but on his return he was again attracted hither, and built his hermitage over the relics of his only love. So did Father Ralf confess him, and by means of the hoard he left behind, Masses for the soul of Julien de Clifford continued to be said in Kendal Church till the period of the Reformation.

I suppose it makes a good enough story, but I do not believe a word of it, and there is one annoying inaccuracy in the matter of the cockleshell upon his broad flat hat, for this proves that the pilgrim had not been to the Holy Land at all but to the great shrine of St James at Compostella in Northern Spain, not that it makes much difference!

One thing the persecuted anchorite never did, I suspect, was dance around the maypole, but that was done in Kirkland. The maypole was set in the road opposite the Wheat Sheaf Inn, and when they were laying the gas main in 1825 the workmen dug up the stone base of the maypole. Although a development from pagan festivals, the custom of gathering round the maypole, of dancing at the great feasts of the Church's year, particularly at Whitsuntide, was considered by the Church to be a healthy occupation. In Kendal the custom continued until 1792, and it was held always in the same place until with the increase of carts, coaches and carriages the maypole was taken down. It is thought that dances were later held in the Vicar's Fields.

I mentioned the Wheat Sheaf, but there are other fine inns in Kirkland like the Ring o'Bells and the Cock and Dolphin, but the Cross Keys, and the Old Ship Inn have gone. In passing, it was half way between the Ring o'Bells and the church gate that the stocks were set up. In 1816, Nathan Sandwich, of Kirkland, spent six hours in these for being drunk on several Sundays in a row. Poor fellow, he would not even have been able by that date to have watched the maypole dancing from his 'secure' position, though the maypole was still there when, in 1776, Isabel Lowis was arrested in Kirkland for stealing a red cloak worth tenpence from Anne Garnett. She pleaded Not Guilty and asked to be tried by jury. The jury brought in a verdict of Guilty and she was imprisoned in the House of Correction in Stricklandgate. At noon the following day she was 'brought to the Chapel stairs,

The River Bela joins the Kent Estuary opposite Whitbarrow
The auld grey town – Kendal

also in Stricklandgate, and then publicly whipped from thence to the Maypole in Kirkland and afterwards discharged'.

A few days later Isabel was in trouble again. The Constable arrested her and took her again to the prison, but two of her friends, Miles Wilson of Kirkland, a butcher, and Daniel Tomlinson, a tailor, 'well knowing the said Isabel Lowis so to be in custody, with force and arms did unlawfully break down, prostrate and lay open the wall of the said House of Correction, to wit, two yards by means whereof they did unlawfully rescue and set at large the said Isabel Lowis'. It must have been good to have such powerful friends!

4

Kendal – The Wool Town

The Kendal archers, all in green
Sir Walter Scott

Kendal's motto is the Latin 'Pannis mihi panis', Wool is my Bread, and there is little doubt about Kendal's importance in the history of the wool trade in England. There was a tradition, now discredited, that a Flemish merchant, John Kemp, had settled in the town during the reign of Edward III, and that the Kendal wool trade owed much, if not all, to him. It is true that Kemp came to England in 1331 from Ghent, and was encouraged by the King, who gave him a 'Letter of Protection', to set up his business in this country, but it seems the place he chose was Norwich and not Kendal! There is absolutely no evidence of any kind that he ever came to Kendal, and so the wishful thinking of earlier writers about Kendal should now be ignored. However, Flemish weavers did come into the district and, in fact, one of the five aisles in Kendal Parish Church is still known as the Flemish Aisle as a result. Flemish weavers came over to this country in their hundreds after the riots in Bruges which culminated in the bloody street massacre of 1349. It was an ominous year if ever there was one, for the Black Death was to wipe out about half the population of the country. Nevertheless, it is thought that a group of Brabanters settled in Strickland Roger, north of the town, at about that time.

The wool trade, however, was well-established long before any Flemings thought of settling in this country. It is known, for instance, that the Cistercians of Furness Abbey were exporting wool to the Continent by sea from their small port on Walney Island by the end of the twelfth century. The abbey had something like two dozen farms or 'granges', many of them fairly isolated in the fells, so isolated, in fact, that the monks used to bring their vast flocks down to the more temperate climate and flatter land of Walney Island for the winter. It has been estimated that there may have been as many as 15,000 sheep altogether in the flocks of these abbey farms. The other Cumbrian monasteries also profited from wool, and managed farms in the Kendal area, like Shap Abbey, for instance, which held land in Longsleddale.

Although much of the wool would go for export, and we know that itinerant Italian merchants were often in the district to inspect the fleeces destined to go abroad, some would inevitably be kept for home use to be spun and then woven into cloth. From this were made not only monks' religious habits but also blankets and clothing for the people of the dales themselves. Up to the time of the granting of the Kendal Charter in 1576 or 1575, according to the old calendar, all wool was spun and woven in the houses of the Kendal townships, all twenty-four of them, although as with any endeavour there arose men with organizing ability who would employ others. These 'clothiers' would likely own the fulling-mill and work a team of carders, spinsters, weavers, shearmen and dyers, not to mention the children who would be useful in sorting the wool at the early stages; they were known as spullers.

I would imagine that most people will be reasonably familiar with the processes of spinning and weaving, but that some, like me, will be less familiar with fulling and dyeing. I have made several references to fulling-mills in the preceding chapters, but what was this fulling process?

When cloth had been dyed it had usually lost some of its strength. This was not the fault of the dyer or of the dyeing process, but prior to dyeing the cloth had to be cleaned or, as it was called, 'bowched', a process which removed much of the lanolin from the wool. The cholesterin-fatty matter which gives the wool 'body' had been washed out of the cloth by boiling it in soapy water. Fulling was a restorative process. The earliest fullers used to 'walk' or tread the cloth in long troughs of soapy water enriched with potash obtained from burning nettles, thistles, or best of all, as Mr Davies-Shiel has argued, green brackens. Soon the fulling-mill took over from the 'walkers', though they were to remain a common enough surname, and, no doubt, some cloth continued to be fulled in the old way; but the mill wheel worked large hammers that beat and pounded the cloth in its soapy bath. Then the cloth would be washed in clear, clean water to remove all the soap, which is why the clothiers needed so much water at their disposal. After washing the lengths of cloth, which would by now have shrunk from their original woven length, they were hung up to dry and shrink further on what were called tenters. These were wooden frames to which the cloth was fixed with tenter-hooks, which is where the phrase 'to be on tenter-hooks' comes from! The man whose job it was to watch the weather and see that the cloth was drying successfully was known as a tenterer or lister. There must have been literally hundreds of tenters to be seen by the Mint, Sprint and Kent in the days of Kendal's prosperity, and many of the sites are familiar names today. There are Tenterfield, Tenter Bank and Tenterholme, to name but three. While the cloth was on the tenters a constant watch was necessary, for much filching went on, so much so that in 1582 the Burgesses of Kendal ordered a special watch to be kept on the tenters after they had received complaints of heavy losses.

Once the cloth was dry there were two main ways in which it could be treated: it could be roughed-up so that the fluffy effect was maintained, or it could be cropped to remove the fluff. The latter process was where the master-craftsman, the shearman, was needed. The shearman, sometimes known as a cropper or napper, removed the fluff or nap of the cloth with an enormous pair of shears, which were often six feet in length, and weighing forty pounds needed two men to hold them steady.

It was the development of the fulling process and the expert dyeing that was to make Kendal famous, and cloths from other parts of the country were often brought to the town for these processes. However, it seems that in the early days the wool of the district was considered inferior, and in 1390, it was described as 'the worst wool within the Realm.' The term 'Kendal cloth' was used to denote any course woollen cloth, and those that sold it were often termed 'Kendalmen'. A Thomas Lambard, of Skipton, was described as a 'yeoman, draper, kendilman, husbandman or clothier', and in 1510, Thomas Pennyington, of Sayles-in-Furness, as a 'Kendilman, clothier or carrier'. However, when Katherine Parr presented her prospective husband a coat made of Kendal cloth are we to suppose that Henry VIII was insulted? Not at all, it seems, for the King felt himself honoured and 'Gave the messenger 4s. 8d. for himself and ordered another coat, and also a doublet for Patch, his Fool.'

Perhaps the King was being kind, but I do not think so, although it is true that 'Kendal' or 'Kendal green' does crop up in literature as a term to imply an inferior kind of cloth. In *Henry IV Part I* Shakespeare has Falstaff tell Prince Hal after the skirmish on Gadshill:

> But, as the devil would have it, three misbegotten knaves, in Kendal green came at my back and let drive at me: for it was so dark, Hal, that thou couldst not see thy hand.

Of course, one of the 'misbegotten knaves' had been Prince Hal himself, but Shakespeare does not explain how in such darkness Falstaff was able to recognize Kendal green; it might have been Sherwood green for all he knew! What Shakespeare is saying is that the men were dressed in the typical clothing of the poorer folk. Some few years after the death of Chaucer, the poet John Lydgate tells of a pauper in his 'threadbare coat of Kendal green', and it was handed down that the Kendal bowmen at the Battle of Flodden Field, some three hundred of them, were wearing some kind of uniform made from local cloth, a fact Scott was able to use in the *Lay of the Last Minstrel*, a line from which I have quoted at the head of this chapter. No doubt there are more references in literature of which I am unaware. However, these examples show that Kendal cloth 'got about', and we should not be surprised that there were Kendal chapmen selling their cloth at Sturbridge Fair, near Cambridge, or that the accounts of the Cloth Hall at Southampton for the year 1552/3 should list the names of at least twenty-five Kendal wool merchants, though the first record of Kendal dealers at the port is dated 1492.

Kendal green, which still catches the imagination, was probably a very special dye prepared from the local gorse or 'whin', the *Genista tinctoria*, often referred to as 'dyer's broom'. This provided the yellow, and then the cloth would be dipped in a blue dye extracted from blueberries or elderberries. It seems to have been a distinctive colour in its early days, a deep shade of green, more blue than yellow, though later the shade was imitated generally.

The Borough of Kendal

The year 1575 was an important one for Kendal for it marks the beginning of the modern town's development. The Royal Charter was issued by Queen Elizabeth in 1575 by which Kendal was incorporated, and the government of the town was entrusted to one alderman, one recorder, twelve burgesses, and twenty-four assistants, known collectively as 'The Alderman and Burgesses of the Burgh of Kirkbie-in-Kendal'. The first recorder was one Robert Briggs, though he seems to have been replaced a year later, and the first Alderman was Henry Wilson, both these names appear on the charter. The office of alderman was held by the Chief Magistrate of the borough, who remained in office for one year only. This first charter remained in force until it was confirmed with other privileges added in 1636, during the reign of Charles I. By this second charter, the first Mayor of Kendal, Thomas Sleddall, was appointed and held office for one year. Although several mayors enjoyed more than one term of office at different times it has always been an annual appointment. A third charter was granted by Charles II in 1684 which confirmed the second.

The first charter of 1575 applied only to the Borough of Kendal, which meant the town that had grown up on the north side of Blind Beck. It did not apply to Kirkland, neither did it apply to the twenty-four townships of Kendal Parish, a fact that was to have important repercussions. Ostensibly, the purpose of the charter had been to preserve standards, since practices of 'insufficient and deceitful dressing and finishing of cloth' had begun to creep in. Particularly the charter was designed to help the young apprentices, but in effect it came to be used to change the whole nature of the wool trade in the district, restricting the use of the term 'Kendal cloth' to cloth woven and prepared within the confines of the borough to the exclusion of the outlying townships. This meant that there were many restrictive practices and only those who were *persona grata* were allowed to trade in the borough; but as intended the borough grew in importance from the time of the charter onwards, and, indeed, though it says little for the morality of it, the seventeenth century was to see a boom in Kendal's trade.

It was at about this time that the term 'Kendal coatings' or 'Kendal cottons' was applied to a cloth which was roughed-up to look like cotton. This cloth was used to dress the first slaves in the West Indies. In 1607 slaves in Barbados are reported to have been wearing Kendal cottons. A few years before, Kendal had suffered a frightening outbreak of the plague when 2,500 people in the parish died. This was in 1598, the year after a statute was brought in to reform abuses in the northern wool trade, 'especially the overstretching of cloths on tenters by means of winches,' and the local Justices of the Peace were ordered to appoint special 'searchers', to punish offenders and destroy all 'prohibited contrivances'. Perhaps, the 'searchers' found the task beyond them, for another statute of 1609 stated that the act of 1597 did not apply to 'Kendals and other course things of like nature and made of the like course wool.'

Over the years Kendal's prosperity increased, and with the expanding trade to the new colonies there was an ever-growing demand for Kendal cottons, so that by the middle of the eighteenth century many fortunes had been made. As a result larger houses had been built and the town had greatly increased in size. In 1770, the Liverpool Custom House books show that some 4,000 cloths, each about 20 feet in length were exported to America and the West Indies, with Virginia and Maryland taking 2,693 between them, and Jamaica 810 cloths. However, as fashions changed and the Colonies developed their own industries, and real cotton, picked by slaves wearing their Kendals, no doubt, was shipped back to England for spinning, the need for Kendal cottons diminished and, as Cornelius Nicholson writing in 1832 in his *Annals of Kendal* says, 'the celebrated Kendal Cottons at length became degraded to the use of horse-checks, floor-cloths, dusters and mops.' It seems as though a 'clean sweep' was inevitable. However, Kendal was fortunate, for as the weaving industry dwindled so the knitting industry began to expand, and the town became the major market in the district for hand-knitted stockings. Wool would continue to be the Kendal man's bread.

Daniel Defoe noticed in 1724 that 'at Kendal and Kirkby Stephen and such places in the country as border on Yorkshire'

Beetham Hall

everybody was knitting. 'The knitting trade is a very considerable manufacture of itself and of late mightily increased,' he wrote. Earlier, in 1671, another Daniel, Sir Daniel Fleming, had said of little Kirkby Stephen: 'This Town is much improved by the Trade of Stockings.' In his *Tour to the North* published in 1770 Arthur Young, the author of *Annals of Agriculture* which extended to forty-seven volumes, had time to note that 'Kendal is famous for several manufacturies: the chief of which is that of knit stockings, employing near five thousand hands by computation.'

Wool was taken by packhorse from the centre in Kendal to the outlying dales where it was spun and knitted into stockings, and these were taken back to be sold in the market in Kendal. At the height of the stocking industry, when thousands of pairs of regimental hose were needed for the troops serving in the Napoleonic Wars, my own valley, Ravenstonedale, knitted 1,000 pairs of stockings a week for the Kendal market, while Sedbergh and Dent produced 840 pairs between them, and Orton 560. That was some knitting. It was Robert Southey who wrote: 'They're terrible knitters a' Dent', but he would have discovered greater wonders at Ravenstonedale!

In 1829, five years before Southey made the Dent knitters famous, Kendal had twelve hosiery dealers, though in ten years the number had dwindled to four through lack of demand and the introduction of machinery. Nevertheless, there were other industries which would soon become important in the town, as we shall see, and I have not breathed a word about shoes or leather yet! First, we must look at the lay-out of the borough itself.

The Auld Grey Town

The Borough of Kendal, like Kirkland, grew up on the west bank of the river where the Kent takes a serpentine course; curving first eastwards then westwards before righting itself and continuing due south by Kirkland. On a map the line of the river looks like a reversed letter S. Of the eastward bulge the townsfolk were able to take full advantage, for it provided an extra parcel of land east of the main street which would become the 'busy' part of the town with two bridges, one much older than the other, bringing traffic in from the east. The main street

Levens Hall
Sizergh Castle

extended northwards from Kirkland and the Blind Beck, running parallel with the general course of the river and situated a little higher up the fellside.

Kendal is built of the local limestone, which is more grey than white, and greyer, for instance, than the Orton limestone to the north-east. When it is wet it looks very grey indeed, so that Kendal is justly called the 'auld grey town', and where the stone has oxidized or become grimed with age it might even be the 'auld black town'. I must admit that walking about Kendal on a drizzly day is one of the more depressing experiences, and one longs for some warmth of colour. Even Kirkby Stephen is saved by the rosiness of the brockram of which it is built, a rock composed of chips of limestone in a cement of red sandstone, but Kendal has nothing like that. O for the 'rustiness' of Penrith, Appleby and Carlisle positively perky in their sandstone smugness! When will pasty-patchy Kendal blush? 'Give me the sun', she says. 'Give me the sun, and I will show you that even grey may smile.'

Highgate

The main street is now known as Highgate, the 'chief street', though it was originally called Soutergate, the 'shoemaker's street', and nothing to do with the 'south', as has been suggested. Considering the fame shoes have brought to the town, for K Shoes are, surely, known by millions who know nought of Kendal, it seems the old name should be resumed:

However, Highgate or Soutergate is the main street whatever one calls it. It begins at the bridge which crosses the beck from Kirkland and continues northwards rising slowly uphill, so that one cannot see from one end of the street to the other because of the brow of the hill, but before 1803 there would have been something else in the way. Highgate leads into Stricklandgate and one might wonder why what appears to be one long street should suddenly change its name. The reason is simply: for three centuries there was a large, long building, known as the New Biggin, the 'new building', at the north end of Highgate separating the two streets. It is still easy to see where this was because the street becomes very much wider just opposite the Town Hall by the corner of All Hallows Lane. The New Biggin had been built largely of wood in about 1500, though the exact date is unknown, so it would have been a fairly new building at the time of Katherine Parr's childhood at the castle. It had two storeys and was some thirty yards long and nine and a half yards wide. On the east side there was a row of shops extending out at ground-floor level with a pentroof sloping down from the upper floor. There was access to the two larger streets on either side of the building, the passage on the eastern side being the wider, though only just wide enough for vehicles, while no cart could have passed through on the western side which had a very narrow cobbled street.

Modern Kendal looks vastly different from the town of even thirty years ago, and many people have complained to me of the difference. We are fortunate to be able to see from early photographs what the place looked like in the latter part of the nineteenth century, but prior to that a lively imagination is necessary if we are to have any idea of how the place looked at all. However, I should think that the removal of the New Biggin in 1803 must have made a great difference to the 'look' of the place and, with the demolition in 1870 of the old Pump Inn at the head of Finkle Street, a little further northwards, marked, from the 'oldy-worldy' point of view, the 'beginning of the end'.

Speed's map of Kendal shows that the famous 'yards', which in the eighteenth century were such a distinctive feature of the town, were very much later on the scene than has often been thought. One thing seems certain and that is that they were not built specially to protect the Kendal folk from the ravages of the marauding Scots, for the Scots had ceased to be a threat of any kind after 1745. As Kendal does not play football with any clubs from over the Border, it seems they will not be much of a threat ever again!

The main purpose of building the yards was to enable an expanding population to make the best use of the river. Had a series of streets been built parallel with the main street and the river, only the street next to the river would have benefited, but by building the yards, which are really small alleyways, diagonally from the main street, with every yard leading down to the water's edge, everybody could use the river for their purposes, dyeing, tanning, fulling, and so on. These yards were like very narrow streets, often leading into a wider area, not quite wide enough to warrant the term 'square', but allowing a small row of houses to be built back slightly from the main passage. Most of Kendal developed on this pattern, and, although the first yards were probably the ones on the eastern side of Highgate, the same pattern was soon followed on the other side of the street, where the passages led up to the fellside and, indeed, became known as Fellside. If one hunts about, it is still possible to gain some idea of what Kendal looked like, and one or two yards have been specially preserved. The finest example is known as Dr Manning's Yard, though it was formerly known as Braithwaite's Yard or simply Yard 83. In this small space George Braithwaite ran his drysalting business until his death in 1812. The Braithwaites were a well-known Quaker family, one of the many in the town, and they seem to have shared the yard with several other businesses, including a dyeworks, a rope-making works and a bark-mill. Every yard in Kendal might have had a fascinating tale to tell had it been allowed to remain to tell it, but most of the yards have been cleared away.

On the west side of Highgate, and giving a certain dignity to an otherwise dull row of houses, is the gatehouse to Sandes Hospital and Almshouse. This was the gift of Thomas and Katherine Sandes in 1659. Thomas Sandes was a shearman dyer who had done very well for himself, eventually becoming a dealer in Kendal cottons. He had been appointed Mayor of Kendal for the year 1647–8 but his benefactions had come later, as the indenture states:

> Whereas the said Thomas Sandes hath saved a considerable share of his temporal estate by buying and selling of woollen cottons commonly called Kendal cottons and being mindful to set apart one convenient dwelling house within Kirkby Kendal for the use of eight poor widows, to exercise carding, spinning of wool, and weaving of raw pieces of cloth for cottons called Kendal cottons; and for the use of a schoolmaster to read prayers to the said widows twice a day, and to teach poor children till prepared for the free school of Kendal or elsewhere.

Sandes went on to stipulate that the widows must be of 50 years old or upwards and should be selected as follows: three from Stricklandgate, three from Stramongate and Highgate, one from Strickland Roger and Ketel, and one from Skelsmergh and

Patton. The last two places were specially provided for in the event of there being no widow available to take up the place, in which circumstances the trustees were to select 'a single woman of good reputation, and a worker of wool, but who should not be allowed to marry'. It would seem to have been all 'work and pray' for the widows, and it is not certain at all that it was an advantage to be an inmate of the hospital, but for some, no doubt, it was a matter of necessity. However, if any widow should be daring enough to consider remarriage she would risk the pain of deprivation, which was fair enough as it would make room for someone else.

The schoolmaster, besides reading prayers to the carding widows, was expected to teach 'poor children'. This was the beginning of the Blue Coat School, founded to prepare boys to go on to the Grammar School, but only after they had learnt to read the psalter. By 1714, there were nine girls at the school as well, taught by one Isabel Fisher.

As the name implies, all the children wore a blue uniform and in 1815 it cost £150 to kit out the 40 boys and 30 girls who that year were in attendance at the school. The school was held in what was known as the Great Room which housed the library, also donated by Thomas Sandes. The Blue Coat School flourished with a fluctuating role of pupils, numbering some 75 when fullest, from its foundation in 1670 until it was amalgamated with the Grammar School in 1886.

The gatehouse to Sandes Hospital has a coat of arms above the gate with the initials of Sandes and his wife together with the date 1659. Inside, there is an alms box with the exhortation 'Remember the Poor Widows', and poor they were certainly considered. In 1784, the magistrates ordered that four recovered stolen gowns should be awarded to four widows at the hospital. Neither were the widows all old, for in that same year Frances Bellingham of Sandy's Hospital, a pauper aged 37, was buried in the parish graveyard.

Today, there is still a row of almshouses in the yard. These were rebuilt in 1852, and even the gatehouse itself has been altered since it was first seen in Highgate. Yet, the hospital remains as a testimony to a 'good' man who having done well in the town turned his thoughts towards those less fortunate, even despite making the first widows work for their keep:

He built for himself a monument.
An almshouse for Poor Old People.

Apart from the many inns in Kendal, which still are many,
though the number had greatly diminished even by the beginning of this century, there were at one time four theatres. One of
these, the Shakespeare Theatre, was situated next to the Sandes
Hospital and behind the Shakespeare Inn. The theatre was built
in 1829, six years after one in Woolpack Yard closed. The first
play-bill announced: 'A Powerful and Efficient Company from
the Principal Provincial Theatres in the Kingdom, under the
management of Mr Stevens, from the Theatre Royal, Manchester.' The first play performed was *Rob Roy*, so the Scots 'invaded'
Kendal once again! After *Rob Roy* there was a 'New Popular
Farce' *The Green Eyed Monster*, and those who know their
Othello will not be surprised that the Moor also boomed out his
woe on this stage, and Hamlet rambled and Lear raged through
the voices of Kemble and Keen, and 'the celebrated actor'
Vandenhoff. What did the Kendalians think of all this? 'Aye, a
droll lad that Shakespeare.' The theatre struggled on for five
years bringing bigger and better names into the town to an
increasingly dwindling audience until, in 1834, the theatre
became a ball-room and billiard-hall. They had not invented
bingo in those days.

It is ironic that this little corner of Kendal is still 'Broadway',
since only a stone's throw away the Brewery Arts Centre gives
Kendal its only theatre, though occasionally mammoth productions are mounted in the Town Hall. The arts centre is converted
from the old Vaux Brewery, and a particularly good architectural job has been done to give excellent facilities to many
different art forms. People sometimes take delight in criticizing
the brewery, but it provides a much-needed stimulus to those
who wish to do otherwise than sit at home in front of the
television. Particularly important, it seems to me, is the work of
the Pocket Theatre based at the Brewery, a group of actors who
take their productions around the Cumbrian villages, performing in schools, halls and clubs.

The arts centre has been open since 1971, and may Kendal
support its work and contribute to its maintenance for many
years to come.

Only two streets lead into Highgate from the west, Captain French Lane and All Hallows Lane. Captain French Lane was once Rotten Row, and is marked as such in Speed's plan of Kendal printed in 1614. Rotten Row derived its name from 'raton raw', meaning a 'row of rat-infested houses', and this familiar English street name occurred in many towns, particularly where there was a stream near to the houses, in this case the Blind Beck. But why change the name to Captain French Lane? I smell a rat. I do not think Captain French was very popular. Although he was churchwarden in 1660, he also took part in the Kaber Rigg Plot three years later, and as an ex-Parliamentary Officer may well have lacked the support of local people once Charles II had returned. French was imprisoned for his part in the rebellion, though he escaped execution, and I suggest that it was the people who allotted the 'rat' his rightful place in the town.

All Hallows Lane is relatively simple. It is named after the Chapel of Ease which used at one time to stand opposite the Town Hall near the New Biggin. Until fairly recently the Public Swimming Baths were in All Hallows Lane, and there are those in Kendal who can just remember the days when women from Fellside used to bring their washing down to the Public Washing House and later hang it out to dry down by the river. The old baths look ripe for demolition!

The present Town Hall is a much extended and altered version of the White Hall designed by Francis Webster in 1825; the work of altering the fine old hall was carried out in 1893. Outside the main entrance of the Town Hall, on the north side, there is a small block of stone, part of the old market cross known as the Call Stone, and once used for 'calling' any notice of importance, particularly royal proclamations and the like. It is easy to recognize the stone for it is usually skirted with empty Tizer tins, spent crisp packets, or the distinctive, yellow fish-and-chip wrapping-papers stuffed behind it. Today, the Call Stone calls one to look away.

Inside the Town Hall there are several very interesting, even 'good' paintings; a little too good perhaps to be left so unguarded. Surely, these should be at Abbot Hall. I am thinking particularly of the *King's Arms Hotel* by Richard Stirzaker, a Lancaster artist, who came to Kendal from his home-town in 1817. The painting shows the King's Arms, a famous coaching inn which was situated in Stricklandgate until it was demolished to make way for Messrs Marks and Spencer; outside the inn is the flashy coach, The Telegraph, the Kendal to Liverpool coach, as it might have looked in 1823.

Also in the Town Hall is another picture by the same artist showing the arrival at Kendal of Lord Brougham for the famous General Election of 1818. Stirzaker shows the crowded street with a lively-looking band blowing their instruments from the top of a coach. This election campaign was to bring considerable publicity to the town, so we should know a little more about it.

The General Election of 1818

Before the Great Reform Bill of 1832 the County of Westmorland was represented by two Members of Parliament, while Appleby, the county town, returned two further members of its own. In this instance it is with the county election we are concerned. In 1818, the two Lowther brothers, Lord Lowther and Colonel Lowther, sons of the Earl of Lonsdale, were standing for the Tories, while the Whigs were represented by one candidate only, Henry Brougham, a brilliant lawyer who was living at the time near Penrith, at Brougham. The lawyer's brief was quite simple: to 'smash' the Lowthers, a mission in which he had the full support of the Earl of Thanet, the High Sheriff of Westmorland, who resided at the family home of the Cliffords, Appleby Castle.

On Nomination Day, which was ominously the 13th of June, all three candidates assembled at Appleby where the Lowthers had been canvassing already for several days, flaunting their bright yellow colours which apart from being their family colour was adopted as the party colour as well. While the voters of Appleby were rallying round the Lowthers, Brougham had arrived triumphantly in Kendal where he had found considerable support, but so few of the Kendalians had the vote that it was not likely to help him much. Nevertheless, he had been loudly cheered when he addressed the Fellsiders from the balcony of the King's Arms Hotel rousing the anti-Lowtherites into a hopeful frenzy, for the Lowthers had never been popular in the borough. At Appleby, Brougham attempted similar tactics, and so did his proposer, Thomas Wybergh, of Clifton Hall.

'Henry Brougham,' began Wybergh, 'is not a courtier: he is not a son of the Lord Lieutenant of the County; he is not the son of a Peer in Parliament; he is not the heir-apparent to large possession and modern-built castles in Westmorland. All the arts of the Lowthers, be they multiplied tenfold, must yield to the spirit of Westmorland yeomen.'

Wybergh's proposing, loaded with sarcasm as it was, was nothing compared with Brougham's opening speech in which he compared the Lowther brothers to toads with yellow stripes and their supporters to sick sheep who were invited to raise up their forefeet if they were able. Yet, in spite of Brougham's eloquence, which was destined to take him far in the future, the result was a foregone conclusion, and although he had gained much support it was hardly enough to beat such massive Lowther support and allegiance.

In Kendal, where Brougham had been liberal with his barrels of free ale, there was such a riot that the distracted Mayor was forced to call in the 15th Light Dragoons to restore order. But this election had brought something into being which is still very much part of our lives, particularly every Friday, for to help them in the fight against Brougham the Lowthers, with the encouragement of Wordsworth, launched a new newspaper, the *Westmorland Gazette*.

The Westmorland Gazette

If the Lowthers had had their way Wordsworth himself would have been appointed the first editor of the paper, but he felt he could not take the job on, although he took considerable trouble to find an editor, a man named Fisher who had experience of journalism in London. Under Fisher's pen the first issue appeared on the 23rd of May, 1818. In its notice to the public the paper announced:

> We hope that we shall never rank amongst the turbulent disturbers of tranquillity, nor amongst the malicious enemies to domestic peace. We know that the Press may be made a great engine of evil in bad hands, but let us hope that ours will never be disgraced by the stamp of infamy.

The paper's motto from the Roman poet, Horace, was printed
beneath the title *The Westmorland Gazette, and Kendal Adver-
tiser*, and translated by the handy couplet:

> Truth we pursue, and court Decorum:
> What more would readers have before 'em?

What more, indeed, but within a very short time there was a
considerable lack of 'Decorum', for Fisher's editorship proving
mild and ineffectual, the pen, or rather cudgel, was picked up by
Thomas de Quincey. De Quincey had been suggested by Wordsworth, though even Wordsworth had some doubts as to the
'Opium Eater's' suitability for the office. 'Whether he is fit, I
mean on the score of punctuality, for such a service remains to
be seen,' he wrote to the proprietors.

Under de Quincey's editorship the *Gazette* shone like a bright
star, and his friends were amazed at the zeal with which he
approached his task, but for the proprietors there were problems: to begin with the editor was hardly ever in Kendal,
preferring to write at home in Grasmere, then there was the
matter of his interests. It was not long before local considerations became tedious to the editor, hardly worth notice compared with wider issues of national importance such as murder,
suicide and peculation. Soon the author of *Murder as One of the
Fine Arts* was treating the Westmorland folk to blood-and-guts
accounts of atrocities committed in Wiltshire and other such
interesting places.

'Last week's specimen is certainly a most blackguard produc-
tion,' wrote the perplexed Lord Lowther. It soon became obvious
that de Quincey would have to go, and realizing the situation
the Editor, himself, handed in his resignation in the November
of 1819.

He had held the post for just sixteen months and had been
thirty-three years old when he began. His salary had been £160
a year out of which he chose to employ a sub-editor to handle the
day-to-day affairs of the paper at two guineas a week. He was
addicted to between 8,000 and 10,000 drops of laudanum a day,
that is, as much as might fill eight ordinary wine-glasses, yet
while editor of the *Gazette* he had also been sending off articles
to *Blackwood's Magazine* and the *Quarterly Review*. He had

made what his friends considered an unfortunate marriage
after he had got a local farmer's daughter pregnant, but his love
for Margaret Simpson was genuine and the attitude of his
friends, particularly that of the Wordsworth women, caused him
great pain, neither in view of Wordsworth's own peccadilloes
was such criticism excusable. Soon after he had accepted the
editor's post he stayed in a small room in the Commercial Inn, a
fairly new hotel built in 1804, in Highgate; at 11 o'clock at night
feeling exhausted and sad he wrote to his wife in tones which
show his feelings:

My Dear Wife, – I have this moment received your note. It has put me
into a little better spirits; for I have been in very bad spirits ever
since I left home. I quitted Grasmere with a heavy heart, and I was
sure I should find nothing in Kendal to comfort me. Indeed, I have
found nothing here but trouble of all sorts. I hope, however, that I
shall soon get the paper into a right train; and the proprietors are
very willing to allow me my own way. The trouble I find is solely
among the inferior people about the press. I am truly grieved to hear
of little Margaret's illness; I hope that it is not the forerunner of
anything worse. God bless her poor little lamb! If you come over
to-morrow in a chaise, I shall be very happy to see you; or if you prefer
next week, I shall be very happy to attend you. God bless you, my
sweet wife! and believe me most affectionately yours,

Thomas de Quincey.

De Quincey never did find anything in Kendal to comfort him,
and, as I have said, it was not long before he was hardly ever in
the place, but the *Westmorland Gazette*, which still serves the
county so usefully, is unlikely to have such an editor again as
the one who wrote: 'A Westmorland sheep, I have already
admitted, is not very conscientious about the rights of property.
In this point indeed, as well as his wit and agility, he resembles
the God Mercury!'

5

The Dance of the Shoemakers

Have I not met you somewhere long ago?
I am all but sure I have – in Kendal church.
Alfred Tennyson

The narrow street opposite All Hallows Lane, which runs eastwards from Highgate by the side of the Town Hall, is Lowther
Street. This was opened in 1781, but it was not long before the
Kendal folk, because of their dislike for the Lowthers, objected
to the name to such an extent that they refused to use it and
insisted on referring to the 'New Street'. Today, however, with
its original name, the street is part of the Kendal one-way
system and is usually so jammed with cars that it is no joy to
walk up or down its narrow pavements. Yet, this one must do to
reach the offices of Gawith, Hoggarth & Co., the makers of the
celebrated Kendal Brown Snuff. The snuff and tobacco industry
had begun at the beginning of the seventeenth century, and
it has been suggested that the plague which hit the town in
1632 was nothing like as virulent as the outbreak of 1598 because of the habit of snuff-taking. Whether this is true or
not, snuff gained a reputation as a 'herba panacea' for all
ills.

Kendal was ideally situated for such an industry to develop,
being only one day's journey by packhorse from the West
Cumberland ports of Whitehaven, Workington and Maryport
where vast quantities of tobacco were imported from the colonies of Maryland and Virginia, which would soon be taking
consignments of Kendal cottons in return.

The first tobacco merchant to succeed in the town was Thomas
Tolson whose name is remembered because of the house he built
in 1683 at Burneside, Tolson Hall. Other merchants soon fol-

lowed his lead; men like Thomas Harrison whose son, also called Thomas, is thought to have been the first snuff merchant to live at No. 27 Lowther Street. It was a Harrison girl, Jane, who had the temerity to elope to Gretna Green with a young Kendal plumber called Samuel Gawith, which is how that famous name came into the Kendal snuff story, for Samuel was eventually forgiven by his irate father-in-law! Then there were the two Henry Hoggarths, father and son both playing an important part in the development of the industry, and the Illingworth family. It was these families who for several generations were to build important companies operating mills at Mealbank, on the Mint, and on the Kent, at Natland, mills which tirelessly pounded away at the tobacco stalks to produce the snuff which would be sent all over the world. As we shall see, there is still snuff being produced at the old mill at Helsington.

Those who walk down Lowther Street will notice the effigy of a Turk perched high on the wall of No. 27. This is a typical snuff-house trade sign and it is thought to have been modelled on the sign of the Turk's Head coffee-house in London, a favourite haunt of Samuel Johnson and his friends. There has been a Turk in Lowther Street since 1870; the original figure disintegrated through age in 1973, but the present figure, carved by Arthur Ayres, was placed by the Kendal Town Council in 1975 to celebrate European Heritage Year. Those heritage years are good for stirring people into action and it was to mark National Heritage Year that the fine restoration of Collin Croft, a yard on the west side of Highgate, was undertaken. It is 'restoration' that is needed rather than schemes intended to 'capture the style and atmosphere of Old Kendal' which do nothing of the sort and seem to demand the demolition of as much of Old Kendal as possible to bring it about. However, I am too late on the scene to make that point; most of the 'damage' has been done already.

If one were to continue down Lowther Street towards the river the way would lead to what is still called 'New Road'. Here one of the chief Kendal bridges, Miller Bridge, is situated. This bridge, at one time called simply the 'Mill Bridge' because it linked the mills on the east side of the river with the town, was originally made of wood, and remained so for centuries. It was to this that Sir Daniel Fleming was referring when, in 1661, he wrote that

'Kendal hath two large stone bridges and one of wood.' However, the wooden bridge was soon washed away by a particularly high flood to be rebuilt on stone piers in 1669, and it was not until 1743 that the first stone bridge was built on the site, but even that has had to be enlarged on several occasions to accommodate the increase in traffic.

Opposite Miller Bridge a narrow street, Kent Street, leads up a steep hill to the point where it meets three other ways: Finkle Street, Stramongate and Branthwaite Brow; but I am never able to begin the climb up Kent Street without pausing to browse in Ewen Kerr's famous bookshop. For many years, long before I had any ideas of settling in the North, I would make a pilgrimage into Kendal to visit Mr Kerr's shop which, when I first knew it in the 1950s, was in Kent Street, and I feel sure that for hundreds like me it has been the focal point of any visit to Kendal before the next stint up the Windermere, Shap or Appleby roads. For my own part, I must thank Mr Kerr for many happy hours, and for keeping in stock just the very books I needed: glancing along my bookshelves it would appear much that came from that shop is with me as I write.

Finkle Street
The earliest reference to Finkle Street I have been able to find is dated 1504 where the name is written 'Fynkelstret'. This strange name is fairly common in the North; there are Finkle Streets in Sedbergh, Thirsk and Stockton, besides the famous one in York, but there must be others, and I seem to remember one in Richmond. The name came possibly from an Old Norse word meaning an 'elbow', for it has been noticed that Finkle Streets are always situated on a hill or where there is a sharp curve of some kind, and in Kendal's case the hill down from Highgate to Stramongate. However, there is another likely meaning, though certainly less attractive, in an Old English word for a heap of rubbish, a dunghill or a corner where rubbish was thrown! When one considers that the fish market was once situated at the top of the hill behind the old Pump Inn, Finkle Street may well be concealing a very niffy past from the days before the cosmetics department of Musgroves wafted its heady promises out into the street, and the browsers in Henry Robert's Bookshop should be thankful that nothing worse than the

comforting whiff of fine, wholesome new books comes between them and their imagination.

There are two very narrow lanes linking Finkle Street with the Market Place; these are the New Shambles and what used to be known as the Old Police Yard because the first police station had been opened there in the 1830s. The New Shambles, however, had been built in 1803 and, as the name tells us, it was here that the butcher's shops were situated. The word 'Shamble' had developed from the Old English *sceamol*, which meant a 'bench for the sale of meat', so it was the display benches outside rather than the shops themselves that gave the name. The former 'butcher's row', though not the first in Kendal, the Old Shambles, had been situated on the west side of Highgate. It had been built in 1779 in the days when all butchers slaughtered the poor beasts in the street and beef was usually 'baited beef' or, if it was not, the butchers were obliged to advertise the fact. Bull-baiting was declared illegal in the county in 1791, although Appleby, where the last bull to face the hounds died in 1812, was slow to give up the custom.

The Old Shambles was inconveniently placed with inadequate drainage so that the blood and urine was inclined to linger about, to say nothing of the offal which was piled up in the street. By the time the butchers moved into the New Shambles the practice of slaughtering outside the shop had ceased, and the animals were taken to the Public Slaughterhouse at Canal Head. The quaint, narrow little lane of the New Shambles is carefully preserved and is certain to remain so.

Finkle Street also has the last of the Brennand's Pork Shops where the Brennand's pork pies are as prized as the famous veal pies of Bellamy, a taste of which was the last wish of an eminent Member of Parliament for Appleby, William Pitt!

For the moment I shall pass by Branthwaite Brow which leads up into the Market Place and continues towards Stramongate.

Stramongate

Stramongate, the 'street of the straw-men', was once the only road from the north-east into the town, and travellers from Penrith or Appleby would approach Stramongate Bridge, which in 1379 was referred to as 'The North Bridge', and today that bridge is still the chief way into the borough.

Stramongate is considerably wider than the other Kendal streets, but it had a similar system of yards leading off on either side, several of which still remain. However, drastic demolition was necessary in this part of the town to construct new roads, so that now Stramongate is split in two with only the upper part free from a constant flow of traffic. One cannot help admiring those towns that have had the courage to keep traffic largely outside. Durham, for instance, is a joy to visit.

It is in one of the Stramongate yards that the Stramongate Primary School is situated occupying much of the site and incorporating along with its modern extensions part of the premises of the Friends' School built in 1698.

The first master of the Quaker school had been John Jopson, and by the time he handed over to Thomas Rebanks the place had flourished to such an extent that a boarding-house was opened in 1728. Rebanks remained at the school for fifty years to be succeeded by George Bewley, a master said to have been 'a man of superior mind and a good classic'. It was on Bewley's retirement that his two cousins, Jonathan and John Dalton, took over the school in 1785. The prospectus of 1787 advertised in the *Cumberland Pacquet* noted:

> The School House is a large and elegant Building purposely erected for the Accomodation of Youth, in an agreeable and airy Situation, and has belonging to it a very valuable Library of Books, chiefly on ancient and modern History, Mathematics, and Natural Philosophy, also an Air Pump, Globes, and several other Philosophical, Mathematical, and Optical Instruments.

John Dalton taught at the school for twelve years and it was while he was at Kendal that he developed his interest in meteorology. It is through his measurements of the annual rainfall that we know that 1792, for instance, was an almost incredibly wet year with 251 rainy days! The following year, perhaps prompted by the weather, Dalton left Kendal to go to the Philosophical Institution at Manchester where he demonstrated the famous Dalton Theory, the Atomic Theory, for which he became widely known. The career of the 'father of modern

St Peter's, Heversham, as a marker for the Shap Fells
Kossowski's ceramic Way of the Cross *in the Church of Christ the King, Milnthorpe*

chemistry' is really outside the scheme of this book, however, for four years Dalton was taught mathematics by a former pupil of the Friends' School of whom I will write at more length. This was John Gough, known as the 'Blind Philosopher'.

John Gough

John Gough was born in 1757, the eldest child of a Kendal shearman-dyer, Nathan Gough, and his wife, Susannah. Nathan Gough claimed descendancy from General William Goffe, who was among the Parliamentary commanders during the Civil War, and one of the regicides. When little John was barely 3 he contracted smallpox so badly that he lost the use of both of his eyes and he remained blind for the rest of his life. His achievement in science, therefore, is all the more remarkable. As a child Gough showed an early aptitude for music and it is said he took lessons from an itinerant fiddler in the town until his father intervened. In his estimation the violin was too sensual an instrument, an attitude difficult for us to understand, but it was one of the absurdities of the time and a sign of the Puritan streak in the Quaker Movement.

Attending the Friends' School was at first difficult for the boy, but he soon began to study botany using his fingertips, tongue and chin in the examination of specimens, and amazingly he could recognize plants he had never touched before, so fully had he understood the descriptions that had previously been read out to him. Among the books Gough had learnt by heart was one by another Kendal man, the *Synopsis of British Plants* by John Wilson.

It was not long before other pupils were coming to Gough for help and he formed a study class in botany, carrying out experiments in his father's dye-house, but he was also proficient in Latin and Greek and had a considerable knowledge of poetry. Whatever Gough thought of the poets, the poets thought highly of him. Coleridge commended him in an essay on 'The Soul and its Organs of Sense', in which he noted: 'The very amiable and estimable John Gough of Kendal is not only an excellent mathematician but an infallible botanist and zoologist, the rapidity of his touch appears fully equal to that of sight, and the accuracy greater.' Wordsworth also paid tribute to Gough in 'The Excursion':

The Cartmel Peninsula from Arnside

No floweret blooms
Throughout the lofty range of these tough hills,
Nor in the woods, that could from him conceal
Its birth-place; none whose figure did not live
Upon his touch.

It was in 1778 that Gough became a resident pupil with the Cumberland mathematician John Slee, at Mungrisedale, where he designed a special abacus with various shapes to enable him to work out algebra. Soon Gough was taking pupils of his own and it was at this time that for four years he taught John Dalton. Later, in 1800, Gough married a girl from Crosthwaite, Mary Harrison, who bore him four children, one of whom was the surgeon, Thomas Gough, who contributed the section on natural history to Cornelius Nicholson's *Annals of Kendal*.

As if his blindness were not suffering enough Gough ended his life with greater difficulties when, in 1823, he developed epilepsy, and the fits became more frequent as time went on so that he died two years later, on the 28th of July, 1825, at Fowl Ing, in Kendal, and was buried in the graveyard of the parish church.

Although, unlike Dalton, Gough did not produce any standard work, he was a frequent contributor to various philosophical and scientific magazines, and among the subjects that interested this remarkable man we should not be too surprised to find: ventriloquism, fairy-rings, and the theory of the speaking trumpet. As Wordsworth said of him:

By science led
His genius mounted to the plains of heaven.

It is only possible to go one way by car over Stramongate Bridge so that many people who visit Kendal will frequently be so caught up in the one-way system as they approach Kendal from the east up Wildman Street that they will miss what is probably Kendal's finest building, the Castle Dairy. This lovely old house is still occupied, and it was built, or rather rebuilt, in 1564. One of the problems with it is that Wildman Street is so narrow that it is impossible to stand back to get a good view of the house, but in its heyday, as part of the castle dairy-farm with fields all about, it was most likely taken for granted much in the same way as it is today.

Wildman Street, formerly known as Wildmangate, has been widened, as have most Kendal streets, though it is still very narrow. On the opposite side from the Castle Dairy there is another attractive old house, Sleddall Hall, and a glimpse through into the yard, Yard No. 3, can quickly take one into the past. At one time there was an inn, the Weaver's Arms, situated here, and later the Packhorse Inn was in the same area. The County Hotel, with its Katherine Parr bar, is at the end of the street opposite the Railway Station. This was once the Railway Hotel, but with the main line station being at Oxenholme some two miles away and the town station being very run down it is easy to see why the name was changed. The Kendal to Winder-mere railway had opened in 1846 and the track and goods yards took up what were once open fields, known as Beezon Fields, and today Station Road crosses over Beezon Road before it becomes Sandes Avenue, all 'new' things that owe their existence princi-pally to the advent of the railway, as does the large building which houses the Kendal Museum.

Kendal Museum has developed recently into a very good show-place indeed. It occupies the old wool warehouse of Whit-well, Hargreaves & Co. which was erected in 1857 in order to be near the railway line. In fact, there was a single track right up to the warehouse loading bay. Besides the usual archaeological 'finds' the museum has an excellent series of natural history show-cases setting the specimens in their typical environment. In the main hall there are portrait sculptures of John Gough and John Dalton, as well as the geologist, Adam Sedgwick, who was born in Dent. Like Abbot Hall the museum charges an entrance fee which unfortunately puts many people off, so that I sus-pect there are many Kendal folk who have never entered the place.

Those who wish to get to know a city or town should approach it on foot, and to this end I sometimes leave my car by the Duke of Cumberland, the first public house I reach as I approach from the Appleby Road. The pub is named after the Duke of Cumber-land, the 'Butcher', who drove Bonnie Prince Charlie back over the Border in 1745. The Jacobites had arrived in Kendal on their march south, but few records were kept of this, unlike the return visit when in full flight the rebels reached Kendal on the 15th of December:

> The country people being there at a market, mobbed their rear, and as they were turning towards the bridge of the town, one of the rebels was killed by a musket fired out of a window; whereupon the townspeople closed in and took two more prisoners. But some shot being fired by the rebels, which killed a shoemaker, an ostler, and another person, the people dispersed.

This account was printed four years after the event in the first issue of *The Agreeable Miscellany; or, Something to Please Every Man's Taste*, an octavo, sixteen-page magazine in a blue cover which served as an advertisement sheet. The *Miscellany*, which is thought to be one of the earliest of its kind, was published by Thomas Ashburner and printed in the basement of what is now Henry Roberts' Bookshop. It lasted for thirty-nine fortnightly numbers, and followed the course of the '45 Rebellion in every issue, the last appearing on the 26th of October, 1750.

The story goes that Bonnie Prince Charlie and Butcher Cumberland slept in the same bed in the town on consecutive nights. It makes a good tale and is possibly true. The house was in Stricklandgate, the home of the Misses Thomson, where the Prince is supposed to have held a levee! Was he really in a fit state for that!

Prince Charles was not the only member of the Stuart family to visit Kendal, if one may use the word 'visit' for his time in the town. In 1617, Charles's great-great-grandfather, James I, spent the night in Stricklandgate on his way from Edinburgh to London lodging at Brownsword House, and it is said the Kendal dignitaries were lacking in their enthusiasm, and their welcome had not come up to their sovereign's expectation of flattery, so instead of bestowing knighthoods on any in the borough James knighted three members of his own household who were accompanying him on the journey.

Although, until modern times, few members of the royal houses actually visited the town, the title Earl of Kendal has been given several times in the course of history: to John Duke of Bedford, the brother of Henry V; John Duke of Somerset, a descendant of Edward III; and John de Foix who was given the title by Henry VI for his faithful service in the French Wars. According to Camden's *Britannia* the Foix family still used the name of Kendal in 1586, and one of the titles Queen Anne granted her husband, Prince George of Denmark, was Earl of Kendal, but he became Duke of Cumberland as well!

However, none of the earls has captured the imagination in the manner of Melusina Erengart von der Schulenberg, Duchess of Kendal. On hearing I was writing a book about Kendal several people said almost accusingly: 'I hope you are going to tell us about Countess Melusina Erengart von der Schulenberg, Duchess of Kendal!' and the name rolls off the tongue in a triumphant fashion, such is the feat of getting her name right. So, even though it is fairly certain she never set foot in Kendal in her life, I shall tell her story.

The Duchess of Kendal

Mademoiselle Schulenberg was *maitresse en titre* to George I, which means she was recognized and accepted as his mistress. She had been born on Christmas Day, 1667, at Emden in Saxony, where her father, Count Gustavus Adolphus, had an estate. The estate was very run down when he took it over but by the time he died in the service of the Elector of Brandenburg, in which he rose to high office, he was able to restore the family fortunes. His son, Matthias, worked for the Venetian Republic and gained a reputation as one of the greatest commanders of the time. He 'did the State some service' as Othello had put it, and was considerably more successful than the Moor.

Melusina was in her way equally talented. She had been fortunate in becoming a maid of honour to the Electress, Sophia of Hanover, and it was at the Hanoverian Court that she first attracted the Electress's son, Prince George Lewis, whose marriage to Sophia Dorothea ended in divorce on account of her alleged infidelity with Count Philip von Königsmark. While Melusina was enjoying the Prince's attentions poor Sophia Dorothea was confined to Ahlden Castle, unable to leave the grounds or receive her friends, and worst of all, she was not allowed to see her children.

Melusina was not with her lover when he landed in England in the September of 1714, though her great rival for his affections, Madame Sophia von Kielmansegge, was. Lady Mary

Wortley Montagu remarked with her usual cynicism that Melusina, knowing how barbarously the English were known to treat their kings, had been afraid George Lewis would have his head cut off within a fortnight! When eventually Melusina did arrive in this country, the Londoners nicknamed her the 'Maypole', for although she had quite a pretty face she was exceedingly tall and gangly. An English assessment of both the King's women was hardly encouraging: 'Ugly old trulls, such as would not find entertainment in the most hospitable hundreds of old Drury.'

Upon both of his mistresses George I showered titles. Melusina, who had become naturalized, started modestly by becoming, in the June of 1716, Baroness of Dundalk, Countess and Marchioness of Dungannon and Duchess of Munster. In March 1719, she moved into the English lists by becoming Baroness of Glastonbury, Countess of Faversham. Not at all a bad beginning, but added to the other titles she was created at the same time Duchess of Kendal, the title by which she chose to be known. Lastly, in January 1723, the Emperor, Charles VI, created her Princess of Eberstein.

Sir Robert Walpole remarked that she would have sold the King's honour for a shilling advance to the best bidder, but there is no doubt that the Duchess of Kendal had considerable influence at Court and great powers of persuasion with her lover. George valued her advice and kept up the custom of transacting state affairs in her apartments. In 1720, Walpole informed Lady Cowper that the Duchess of Kendal's interest did everything; that she was in effect 'as much Queen of England as ever any was.' The King did everything by her.

In the June of 1727, Melusina accompanied the King on the visit to his German dominions from which he never returned. She seems to have decided to remain in Holland while he journeyed on alone towards Osnabrück, where he collapsed in the coach and died a few hours after his arrival. News of the King's collapse was hurried back to the Duchess but she was still on her way to Osnabrück when the news of his death reached her.

George I was buried in Hanover, and the Duchess of Kendal, now a 'very tall, emaciated, ill-favoured old lady' returned to Kendal House, Isleworth. It was there that she thought the soul of the dead King had visited her in the shape of a raven. Perhaps the lover had winged in to see how she was coping with the £40,000 he had left her in his will!

Melusina herself died in the odour of sanctity on the 10th of May, 1743. She had borne George two daughters: Petronella Melusina, Countess of Walsingham, in 1693 (who later married Philip Stanhope, fourth Earl of Chesterfield) and, in 1703, Margaret Gertrude (who later married the Count von Lippe).

In marrying Lord Chesterfield Petronella was only on the edge of fame for she was not the mother of the boy to whom the 'letters' were written, but, in the manner of the time, she would have been aware of the 'natural' son's existence!

Stricklandgate

Both James I and Bonnie Prince Charlie stayed at houses in Stricklandgate, the second most important street in Kendal, which is, today, a continuation of Highgate, and it is only possible now to drive northwards down it.

Stricklandgate, 'the road leading to the stirk land', was often referred to as the 'Drover's Road', nevertheless, it was the first street in Kendal to be made-up and the first street in the country to be macadamized. John McAdam, a Scotsman from Ayr, had become involved in the work of the Cumberland and Westmorland Turnpike Trusts, and his first attempt at his system of road surfacing had been the reconstruction of Stricklandgate, in 1824. Simply, the McAdam method was to lay a hard-core of broken rock with the pieces becoming smaller as the core reached the surface. This is still the method used today, though the introduction of tar as a binding material came later. McAdam had nothing to do with tar, but his name has for ever become associated with it.

Stricklandgate runs down the northern slope of the hill on which the Borough of Kendal is situated, and, as I have said before, it was originally divided from Highgate by the New Biggin demolished in 1803. The Market Place is now open to Stricklandgate, but was until 1909 enclosed with only two small passages allowing access to the street; while at the eastern end it was linked with Finkle Street by Branthwaite Brow, the 'steep clearing' brow; and with Finkle Street again on the south side by the New Shambles which appears as Watts Lane on Speed's map of 1614, and the Old Police Yard just as it is today.

There is a market on Saturdays and a smaller one on Wednesdays. The Saturday market is according to the charter granted to Gilbert Fitz-Reinfred by Richard I, in 1189. It is not nearly as large as many markets of towns of a similar size, and this is principally owing to lack of space. However, in the Market Hall one still sees local farmers selling their produce, which is less usual in other places, and Kendal Market on Christmas Eve, open by special concession, is an exciting sight.

During the week cars are parked down the centre of the square, which seems a pity when there is a vast multi-storey car park so near, but the square is free! Even so, with the sensible use of colour, the Market Place is bright in comparison with much of the town. Outside the Globe, one of the several public houses in the Market Place which are all brightly painted, and in good taste, the borough stocks were once situated, and it was from the steps of the St George's Chapel-of-Ease, which formerly stood in the place of the present War Memorial, that felons, like Isobel Lowis, were whipped all the way down Highgate to the maypole in Kirkland.

It was a great blow to the town when some idiot set fire deliberately to the old Moot Hall, in 1969. This important building had been erected in 1591, and although almost totally remodelled in 1729, it remained in use by the Mayor and corporation until they moved to the new Town Hall, the White Hall, in 1859. The end of the Moot Hall with its square tower is suggested by the present building, now a clothes shop, designed to remind the Kendalians of what they are missing.

Those who walk along Stricklandgate may notice on the east side, near the post office, a fine model of a black bristly boar, the hog trade sign of the Black Hall Brush Factory which used to occupy the house. This house had at one time been the home of one of the first Kendal aldermen, Henry Wilson. However, the Wilsons are not far away, and there may be a whiff of peppermint in the air, for close at hand is the Kendal Mint Cake 'factory' of J. E. Wilson & Sons. Kendal Mint Cake, which is a preparation of sugar, glucose, syrup, salt and oil of peppermint set hard and looking not unlike fudge, has a truly 'global' reputation and has reached dizzy heights! So invigorating has it been found to be that it was taken, perhaps I should say devoured, on the south face of Annapurna during the expedition of 1970, and in 1978 its peppermint freshness was breathed into the icy air at the North Pole.

The Mint Cake is attractively wrapped, sometimes having Lakeland scenes, but the last bar I bought showed an explorer well wrapped against the arctic weather outside his bivouac and holding what looks like a mouth organ, but no doubt it is meant to be a slab of the celebrated white or brown, as hogged in the 'Headless Valley, and crunched on North West Karakoram, Kendal Mint Cake'. However, it was another equally well-known company, Daniel Quiggin & Son, which supplied mint cake for Bonnington's Everest expedition in 1975.

It was on the west side of Stricklandgate that two of Kendal's most famous inns, the King's Arms, and the Woolpack were situated, and the Woolpack is still very much there! Also on the west side was Yard No. 10, known as Redman's Yard because Christopher Redman, an alderman of the borough, had his cabinet-making business there. Redman became Mayor of Kendal in 1749; but however good a mayor he was he will always be better known for having let premises in his yard to an itinerant portrait artist, Christopher Steele. Contrary to the general view of Steele's talent as a painter, he was a very competent portrait artist and examples of his work show that he was certainly in a position to take in pupils, though possibly his erratic temperament was likely to give them the wrong emotional lead; he eloped with one of his pupils to Gretna Green! However, though Steele remains relatively unknown, one of his pupils was destined to become one of the greatest portrait painters England has ever produced. This was, of course, George Romney.

George Romney

Romney arrived at Redman's Yard in 1755; he was barely 21 years old.

George Romney was the second son of 'Honest John Rumney', a small-time farmer and cabinet-maker whose family had moved to Dalton in Furness from Appleby sometime during the Civil War. It will be noticed that George Romney changed the spelling of the family name, though it is fairly certain he continued to pronounce it in the same way.

It was at the Rumney home in Dalton, Beckside, that George and the other ten children were born. Mrs Rumney, Anne

Simpson, was a Cumberland girl from Sladebank. Young
George attended a boarding-school close by at Dendron, some
four miles from his home, though he seems to have remained
there only for a short while, so that by the time he was eleven he
was working for his father. It is said he made violins which he
decorated with ornamental carvings and, even at this early-
stage, amazed people with his ability to 'get a likeness'. His
earliest attempts at portraits are thought to have been sketches
he did of the workers in the wood shop. This sounds more
credible than another story that he spent hours copying the
inn-sign of the Red Lion Inn he could see directly opposite.
Perhaps he did both, or neither, but whatever the true circumstances of his early attempts at drawing, he showed sufficient
talent for his father to apprentice him to Steele in 1755.

Romney found his time with Steele somewhat irksome and
complained that he was made a drudge, though the hard work
was a good lesson and would stand him in good stead for the
future. Steele seems to have taken Romney into his confidence,
particularly in the matter of his intended elopement. The effect
on Romney, whether from a sense of guilt or sheer excitement,
resulted in a fever and he was forced to retire to bed for several
weeks during which time he ran a high temperature and was
delirious. This illness was to have happy results, or what looked
at the time like happy results; for he was nursed, exceedingly
well it seems, by his landlady's young daughter, Mary Abbott,
and the two fell deeply in love. So strong was the attachment
that when Steele, all newly wed by the blacksmith at Gretna
Green, summoned Romney to York where he had taken up
residence, Romney felt that he could not part from Mary without
making his attachment permanent, so the pair were married in
the parish church at Kendal on the 14th of October, 1756. On the
whole it had been quite an eventful year!

When he left Kendal, Romney set a precedent which he
followed for the rest of his marriage, he left Mary at home; for
her it must have been like being married to an arctic explorer.
Romney remained in York for about a year, assisting his master
with his many commissions including one from Laurence
Sterne, though at that time the author of *Tristram Shandy* was
relatively unknown. There is an unconfirmable story that
Sterne attempted to get the pupil to paint the portrait recogniz-

ing immediately his superior talent. As a matter of fact, at the time, Romney's work was not superior to Steele's.

On leaving York the painters moved to Lancaster, and it was here that Romney decided to sever his connection with his master and proposed that the sum of £10 he had lent his master on a previous occasion should be the price of his freedom. Perhaps Steele was glad not to have to pay back the money, but it is said that he accepted in order 'not to stand in the way of one who, he was sure, would do wonders'. Romney lingered on in Lancaster for a while but soon returned to Mary at Kendal, where, taking his younger brother, Peter, then a lad of sixteen, as his assistant, he set up his own studio. So it was that his early clients were some of Kendal's dignitaries: Colonel Wilson of Abbot Hall and the Rev. Daniel and Mrs Wilson besides the Stricklands of Sizergh and Dr Bateman, the Headmaster of Sedbergh School. When Dr Bateman saw what Romney had made of him he was disgusted and Romney had considerable difficulty in exacting his fee. Looking at that painting today, as it hangs above one of the doors in Powell Hall at the school, one cannot help sympathizing with the Doctor. The portrait is dreadful! In fact, in his early portraits there is little to convince one of Romney's genius, but that he had, hidden, pent-up, waiting to spring.

The fee for a full-length portrait was six guineas, and two for a three-quarter length, and during the three years he spent in Kendal he prepared himself for the great test to come, in London. He managed to raise a little money by raffling twenty-five paintings in the Moot Hall at 10s. 6d. a ticket. In saying this took place in the Moot Hall I am accepting tradition, though I think it unlikely that the corporation would have allowed the hall to be used for such purposes. More likely it all took place outside in the market.

Romney arrived in London some time during 1763 and took lodgings near the Mansion House, in Dove Court, though he later moved to Bearbinder Lane. He had about £50, that is, half of what he had raised through the raffle, the other half he had left with his wife.

The first painting he executed in London was his *The Death of General Wolfe* with which he won a prize from the Society of Arts. It has been suggested that Romney was considered for the second prize of 50 guineas, but that the decision was reversed owing to the intervention of Joshua Reynolds. Whether this is true or not, one of the trials of Romney's life was that he had to endure the back-biting jealousy of Reynolds. This was entirely one-sided and Romney did absolutely nothing to deserve it except paint a little too well.

In 1764, Romney travelled abroad for the first time, visiting Paris where he spent hours copying the paintings in the Orleans Gallery. Now, sadly, it is beyond the bounds of this book to relate in very much detail the time Romney spent in Paris, London, or anywhere else, except Kendal. During his time in London he rose to be one of the most respected portrait painters of his day, painting many of the eminent people of the time, including Wesley, Gibbon, William Pitt and Edmund Burke, besides innumerable beauties, of which the most noted was Emma Hart or, as she is better known, Lady Hamilton. I think I must say something about her!

Romney first met Emma in 1782 and besides painting her in her own character, she was to model for him in all kinds of classical, biblical and Shakespearean poses. The Prince of Wales, the future George IV, paid Romney 100 guineas to paint Emma as Mary Magdalene and Calypso. No doubt Emma leapt from one pose to the other with abandon. She was certainly Romney's chief source of inspiration: 'My dear Sir,' she wrote to him soon after her marriage to Sir William Hamilton from Naples, 'my friend, my more than father.' What is one to make of that? Such addresses have led some to think that there was some kind of an affair between the painter and his model; that Romney was infatuated is undeniable, but the relationship seems, on what little evidence there is, to have been platonic only.

What is known is that some time during 1776/7 Romney painted the charming Gower family, and 'they' are now in Kendal, as indeed was the painter at the close of his life. He had painted literally hundreds of portraits: 'I have made many grand designs,' he wrote towards the end to his son, Rev. John Romney, 'I have formed a system of original subjects, moral and my own.' It was as though the 'work' was done, the hideous and the beautiful faces gone; those who had sat for him, who had paid him, whom, in many cases, he had 'made' beautiful though they lacked it in their faces and their lives, had all faded away. Was he now able, at last, to begin? He would paint a Milton gallery, just as he had painted a Shakespeare one. 'Hence it is my view,' he wrote, 'to wrap myself in retirement, and persue these plans, as I begin to feel I cannot bear trouble of any kind.' It was summer in Hampstead, and without saying a word to anyone he set off for home, for Kendal. His sight was failing; he experienced frequent fits of dizziness, and numbness in his fingers of late had made it almost impossible to hold a brush. Mary received him with joy and sympathy, she had nursed him in his youth, she was ready to do so again. His health was fast failing, his mind going; when one of his brothers, James, came to visit him there was no sign of recognition. Mary watched and waited for two years, and she held him when he died as helpless as a baby on the 15th of November, 1802.

Romney was not buried in Kendal. His body was taken back to Dalton, the place of his birth, although there is a monument to him in Kendal Church. Do not go to look at that before you have seen the Gower Family in their swirling dance, all you shoemakers! Go and join the dance! Go where Romney lives!

6

The Lyth Valley

The damson's abloom, it blows so slight,
Like a young lamb in a spring dawn.
Margaret Cropper

Two small rivers, the Gilpin and the Pool, meet each other in what is known as the Lyth Valley, 'the valley of the hill', and the Gilpin, being slightly the larger, continues southwards to meet the Kent at a point some three-quarters of a mile before it opens out into its estuary between High Foulshaw and Halforth. As the valley is at sea-level, until it was drained, it was usually flooded for most of the year, though there seems from earliest times to have been some kind of a causeway across it, which took the form of an embankment constructed on tree-trunks kept into place by poles driven into the boggy earth. Today, although the valley is still inclined to slight flooding after very heavy rainfall, the efficient system of dykes soon takes control and the Gilpin and the Pool have learnt that any efforts on their part towards grandeur are quickly thwarted.

The fact that for much of the time there was no definite river running through the valley is almost certainly the reason why the valley is named after the hill and not the river; for Lyth is the Old Norse word *hlith*, which meant a hillside, but we will have to guess which hillside is meant for there are two spectacular contenders to choose from: Scout Scar, on the east side of the valley, nearer Kendal; and Whitbarrow Scar, on the west side. Tradition seems to favour Whitbarrow Scar, and the region just north of the Scar with the small village of Crosthwaite has for long been known as Crosthwaite and Lyth.

Each of the Scars that 'guard' the Lyth Valley are exhilarating for walkers, and I know of no better way to see the magnificent landscape of southern Westmorland than to walk either of them. For my own part, I have tended to favour Scout Scar, but this is probably because it is easier for me to reach, and nearer my home. The view from Scout Scar is breathtaking, and often in more senses than one, since I have sometimes experienced such fierce winds up there that it has been difficult to breathe at all! All about there are glories: the Lake mountains to the north, which, if there is snow about and the day is clear, appear to be a few yards away. There have been days when those mountains have seemed to be lined up like an army awaiting to invade the Auld Grey Town, though sometimes they are as remote as Greenland; then to the west Whitbarrow Scar, a sister ship in the convoy making for the Kent Estuary, and, if the tide is out with the sun shining, the vast silver desert of Morecambe Bay away to the south; however, perhaps loveliest of all, but I am biased, are Benson Knott above the town to the east, and beyond, the Howgills and their rounded secrets, for I am not a craggy wanderer though there be crags a'plenty. Where the great glacier artist has tooled and plained, mine are to walk not climb!

The River Gilpin
The Gilpin rises at a point some two miles east of Bowness-on-Windermere where two separate streams run by, or through, Gilpin Park plantation. As one stream, the Gilpin continues due south for a while as far as Crosthwaite where it soon changes course slightly, running in a more easterly direction parallel with the Bowness road, the damson trail, the A5074. Then, entering the Lyth Valley, it continues southwards to meet the River Pool, as I have already described.

The origin of the Gilpin's name is obscure, and it may well be named after the Gilpin family which, besides being associated with Kentmere, was an important Westmorland family from the thirteenth century onwards. If this is so it is unusual. With the course of the river being for so long ill-defined it is possible that the river was known in its upper reaches as Gilpin Beck. The earliest record I have seen spells the name 'Gylpyne', which is so like the later spelling that it tells us nothing. However, there is a Frisian word *gulp*, meaning a flush of water or a stream, as opposed to the normal English use of that word which is, of course, onomatopoeic and was first used in the sixteenth century. This could have something to do with it.

The only village actually built around the banks of the Gilpin is Crosthwaite, and unlike the name of the river that of this pleasant little hamlet is easy: it means, simply, 'the clearing with a cross'. This Crosthwaite should not be confused with the larger parish of that name situated further north and containing within its bounds many of the 'glories', so called, of the Lake District. The possibility of such mistaken identity has meant that the Gilpin Crosthwaite was usually linked with Lyth so that the parish, though now united with Cartmel Fell, Witherslack and Winster, was for long known as Crosthwaite and Lyth, although it was a chapelry of Heversham. Crosthwaite and Lyth included the hamlets of Bowland Bridge, Crosthwaite Green, How, Hubbersty Head, Pool Bank, Raw and Tarn Side, while what is now the village was Crosthwaite Church Town, often referred to, simply, as 'Town'.

At Crosthwaite Church Town the Angles probably set up one of their crosses, for, as we shall see, there was an Anglian monastery at Heversham in the ninth century. It is known that in the thirteenth century there was a chapel at Crosthwaite dedicated to the Blessed Virgin Mary which is mentioned in a document of about 1200. In fact, for such a remote area Crosthwaite is particularly rich in documents; we learn, for instance, that in 1390 John de Hall held a fulling-mill for which he paid an annual rent of 6s. 8d.; and, at about the same time, Robert Philipson paid the higher price of £2 for the corn-mill. Both the mills were, of course, on the Gilpin. However, the most interesting document of all records how the inhabitants of Crosthwaite and Lyth 'ought to place themselves in their parochial Chapell for ever'. This document is dated 1535, and gives a complete list of the inhabitants, men and women, and the positions in the rows of pews they were to occupy with the warning: 'Men and women that break this order are lyable to the penalty of 6s. 8d. one half to the chief lord, and the other half to the church.' One may see that the fine was the equivalent of the rent paid for the fulling-mill for a year, which would have stung the pocket, or the purse! There is one delightful detail, however, of which we will never guess the true meaning. Mrs Garnett is singled out in the document, and is ordered to kneel or sit in her form next the

The village green, Natland

wall. Was it a case of the weakest going to the wall? One would like to think so, for that is the origin of the phrase, or, perhaps, the poor woman was being ostracized in some way. Was she, I wonder, young or old; was she a 'naughty' young wife, or an old crone? We shall never know, all we do know is that she was to be by the wall, for ever!

About two miles south-west of Church Town is a seventeenth-century house of three storeys built on to an earlier pele tower; this is Cowmire Hall. As pele towers go this one appears to be very late and it had been described as the last to be built in Westmorland. The name of the hall is not as uninviting as it sounds, since the cows were very little ones. The earliest record, written in 1332 spells the name 'Calvemeyer', the 'calves' marsh'.

Cowmire was owned by the Briggs family in the sixteenth century, the family which endowed the church on Cartmel Fell. In the east window of that delightful little church there is a strange, scarcely readable supplication: 'Wilm brigg goeth to London upon tuesday xith day of April God protect him.' The window fails to tell us whether he ever returned!

Another house situated about a mile or so south of Cowmire is Pool Bank, a farmhouse, built at the end of the seventeenth century by John and Catherine Hartley whose initials are carved over the front door with the date 1693. The house is L-shaped, with the two wings extending to the south and east, and there is a small spinning-gallery above the door at the back of the house.

The River Winster

It has been suggested the Winster takes its name from the Old Norse *vinstri* meaning 'the left', as opposed to the Gilpin on the right. This is assuming that it was the Norsemen who named the river and that they viewed the situation from the south, with Whitbarrow, that great block of carboniferous limestone, being the cause of the division. However, Whitbarrow is, of course, the 'white hill', and it is possible the Winster has the meaning of 'white' also. One professor, noting that white clay had been dredged up from the bed of the river, put me in mind of an early Welsh word meaning 'white', so the Winster may well be the 'white stream'. It rises on the southern slopes of Undermillbeck

A train crosses the viaduct at Arnside
Sunset at Cartmel

Common and gives its name to a small hamlet situated about three miles south of Bowness. In fact, the Winster and the Gilpin rise within about a mile of each other.

The Winster marked the old boundary between the County of Westmorland and the part of Lancashire north of the sands, even though the shores of Windermere might have seemed a more obvious division, at least in the northern part. Flowing almost due south the whole of its twelve-mile course, it eventually meets the Kent Estuary by the village of Lindale, a little east of Grange-over-Sands.

Witherslack
Once a chapelry of Beetham Parish, Witherslack, 'the hollow in the wood', is a small village situated on the south-west slopes of the smaller hills below the Whitbarrow Scar escarpment, on the east bank of the Winster. Witherslack also included the two townships of Meathop, 'the middle plot of enclosed marshland', and Ulpha, 'the place of the wolf'. These are situated along the north bank of the Kent Estuary, and are slightly raised parcels of land in a very boggy area which was for centuries used as the main source of fuel, so that many of the inhabitants were employed in turf-cutting.

However, the main part of Witherslack, which centred on the village, is very different country, hilly, wooded, with roads running along each side of the fell. Before the faster stretch of road from Levens Bridge to Newby Bridge on the Barrow road was built the route used to pass by the Derby Arms, a good place to stop, though now it is easily missed. Over the fireplace in the restaurant is the large head of a stag shot on Whitbarrow Scar just before the First World War, an enormous great beast it must have been. From the inn a short road leads up to the narrow village street where, on the west side, there is a charming little shop with an old-fashioned sign-board which advertises 'Mary Clifton. Grocer'. However, generally speaking, there is not very much at Witherslack to keep one occupied except the surrounding countryside!

The manor was held in early days by the Harrington family, but the Harringtons fought for Richard III at the Battle of Bosworth which happened to be the losing side. The land was forfeited to the Crown and Henry VII granted it to Sir Thomas

Broughton of Broughton Tower in Furness, but Sir Thomas soon
was in trouble for his part in the abortive plot to place the
kitchen-boy, Lambert Simnel, on the throne, and was attainted
of high treason. The king then granted Witherslack to Lord
Stanley, the first Earl of Derby, which accounts for the Derby
Arms. However, things did not go very smoothly for the Stanleys, for the estate was confiscated from them by Cromwell at
the time of the Commonwealth for their royalist sympathies,
and the manor was not restored to them until the reign of
George II.

The church at Witherslack, situated on the west side of the
fell, is dedicated to St Paul and was built largely through the
efforts of John Barwick, who was Dean of St Paul's during the
reign of Charles II. Nikolaus Pevsner described Witherslack
church as 'honest and unpretentious', and like many churches in
the region there is no division between chancel and nave,
though both were heightened in 1768.

John Barwick

Two brothers, John and Peter Barwick, were both born in
Witherslack, but it is with John I am concerned. He was born in
1612, and probably educated at Sedbergh School, founded in
1525, from which he went up to Cambridge at the age of
eighteen. During the Civil War Barwick seems to have acted as
a royalist spy, and even joined the Parliamentarian army at the
request of the King in order to pass back information and report
the army's attitude to the 'King's person'. During this time also,
when it was thought he might be under suspicion, he became a
private chaplain to the Bishop of Durham, and continued to send
messages to the King.

In 1650, after the regicide, Barwick's cover was broken and he
was arrested and thrown into the Tower, where he remained
without trial for two years and, severely tortured on several
occasions, he was kept in solitary confinement for all that time.
However, charges were never brought against him and he was
eventually released.

After the death of Cromwell, Barwick was one who worked
assiduously towards the restoration of Charles II. It was as a
reward for his efforts that the King appointed him Dean of St
Paul's and later offered him a diocese. Barwick refused this,

preferring to remain attached to the great cathedral, said to
have been one of the finest in Christendom. This would soon be
gutted in the terrible fire of 1666 but by then, however, the
newly appointed Dean had been dead for two years. It was in
Barwick's will, dated 1664, that provision was made for the
people of his birthplace. The will noted:

> That Witherslack, the place of my nativity, was four or five miles
> distant from the parish church, and cut off from it by an arm of the
> sea twice a day, which was both troublesome and dangerous for
> passage, especially for burial of the dead.

It seems extraordinary that the dead were borne for such long
distances, and the term 'bearer' had a much more significant
meaning than it does today when it often means lumbering a
coffin on to a trolly! For the folk of Witherslack the hazardous
trips across the sand came to an end when, in 1671, their new
church was built from money granted 'for the purchase, enclos-
ing and consecrating of a parcel of ground for a graveyard' by the
generous Dean.

The career of Peter Barwick was also to take him to London
where he was appointed Physician in Ordinary to Charles II,
and he too granted a small income to Witherslack. These were
the rents from the hall and demesne of Hareskeugh, near
Kirkoswald, in Cumberland.

Levens

I intend to travel eastwards from Witherslack along the A590,
which meets the A6 at Levens Bridge. This road has been
greatly improved, but like all fast roads the tendency is to race
along it and notice little. However, it would be impossible to
ignore the strange chimneys of Nether Levens Hall situated
south of the road and on the north bank of the River Kent. The
cylindrical chimneys are typical of the region and there are
many to be seen in the town of Kendal itself. The house, like the
one at Cowmire, is a sixteenth-century addition to an old pele
tower, and an important pele this one must have been, guarding
the entrance to the river on the north side and matching the
towers of Hazelslack and Arnside on the south. In 1594, the hall
was the home of Thomas Preston, but prior to that it had

belonged consecutively to the Redmans and a family which took the name of the place and called itself de Levens.

Levens, named after one of the early Norse settlers, is 'Leofa's Headland', and the name seems to have been used to refer to the manor, the village of Levens being known as Beathwaite Green until comparatively recently. It was at Beathwaite Green that the present church of St John's was built in 1828, near Causeway End which marked the eastern end of the raised track that passed over the marshes.

Levens is listed in Domesday Book, where it appears as 'Lefuenes', and is included among the many holdings of Earl Tostig. It is perhaps worth noting that when the survey was taken in 1086 Tostig, the renegade brother of King Harold, had been dead for twenty years having fallen at the Battle of Stamford Bridge! It was the Conqueror who granted Levens to Roger de Poitou, and as we have seen already, he did not remain in favour for long. A hundred years later the manor was divided into two, Over Levens and Nether Levens, and it is at the former that the great house of Levens Hall is situated.

Levens Hall

The de Redman family was one of the most important in Westmorland with several members becoming Knights of the Shire. Richard de Redman became Speaker in Parliament in 1415, the year of the Battle of Agincourt. Besides being involved in government the de Redmans were churchmen; another Richard was Abbot of Shap in 1471, and later went on to be Bishop of Exeter then Bishop of Ely. It was at Ely House, the Bishop's residence in Holborn, that he died in 1505, but his body was taken back to Ely for burial.

Unlike the Redmans, a great family that served church and state, the next owners of Levens, the Bellinghams, although an old family, were among those that sought to 'get rich quick' on the dissolved monastery estates. There is little doubt where the money came from to purchase Levens, though the last Bellingham to own the place was forced to sell up to pay off his gambling debts in 1688!

It was Alan Bellingham who bought Levens from the Redmans some time during the 1570s, but he was unable to take possession because the widow of Sir Richard Redman had insisted on staying on, even though she had been widowed a second time when Sir John Preston, her second husband, died a few years before her. So it was Sir Alan Bellingham's son, James, who eventually lived in Levens Hall and he was largely responsible for the fine example of late Elizabethan architecture we see today. However, Levens is as well known for its garden as for its architecture and the designing of the garden had come later, when the last Bellingham to own the hall, another Alan, was forced to sell up. The property was bought by a relation, Colonel James Graham, for £24,000. Colonel Graham was the Keeper of the Privy Purse to James II, and after the abdication he employed the royal gardener, a Frenchman named Beaumont, to design the gardens at Levens. Beaumont had trained at Versailles under the most eminent gardener of all, Le Nôtre, and his use of topiary was to make Levens one of the most distinctive gardens in the country. There is a room in the hall known as the Beaumont Room and a portrait said to be of Beaumont is to be seen also.

Colonel Graham, who became Sir James Graham, made certain alterations to the house, particularly the south range, and the brewhouse where the famous 'morocco' was brewed which the Mayor and Corporation of Kendal used to sample on their way back from opening the Milnthorpe Fair on the 12th of May each year. The special brew was particularly potent and it was supposed to be kept for twenty-one years before tapping. It was a dark, blackish-looking ale, hence its name, and there must have been a few sore heads on the morning of the 13th, if the tales of its powers are to be believed; perhaps, it was as prized by the Kendal Corporation as the 'biggest butt' of Rhenish was by the Corporation of Hamelin! So Kent water was not only good for turning creaky old mill-wheels, it could spin a few heads as well. It is said the toast was 'Luck to Levens Hall while t'Kent flows'.

It would be difficult to do justice to Levens Hall in a short space, so now that I have whetted, if not wetted, your appetite, you will just have to go there!

Helsington

The road from Levens village, which leads towards Underbarrow and follows the east side of the Lyth Valley, is one of the most beautiful in the area, particularly in the spring when the wild daffodils are out, for the way passes by Brigsteer which is largely owned by the National Trust. One need not go to the banks of Ullswater or to Dora's Field for daffodils! All this 'host' is in Helsington, a former chapelry of Kendal, though as a perpetual curacy it was always thought of as a parish.

At one time there must have been some barns in Helsington which gave the name to Helsington Laithes. A laith was an English version of the Old Norse *hlatha*, meaning a 'barn' and found in several other place-names, such as Colby Lathes and Laithwaite. I have wondered whether the barns were some kind of store-place for the people of Kendal in early times, but where there were once barns there are now rows of little houses, for Helsington Laithes is today the south-west part of Kendal, sprawled along the Milnthorpe Road and cut through by the A591, the Kendal bypass.

It may be remembered that Sir Thomas Seymour is thought to have rented a property at Helsington Laithes in order to be near Katherine Parr who was living at Sizergh Castle. This was almost certainly Helsington Laithes Manor House, which was greatly altered in the seventeenth century, but it is still a very fine place to look at. The house was originally owned by the Bindloss family, but it would have been none other than Alan Bellingham from whom Seymour would have rented it. Bellingham had bought Helsington from the Bindlosses in 1487, but he was the father of the purchaser of Levens Hall!

There has never been a village of Helsington, 'the farmstead on the col or neck of land'; and the name probably refers to Scout Scar, or the ridge between Holeslack and Brigsteer, a little further south. Although there are many outlying farms, the centre of population, if one may give it such a grand title, has always been Brigsteer.

The first record of the name Brigsteer, dated 1227, spells it 'Bryggstere', and it is easy to see that there is a bridge of some sort in the first syllable while the 'stere' is, as one might guess, a steer or young bullock. It has been suggested that the 'bridge' may refer to a 'hard' or causeway across the marshland, but also possible is the existence of a bridge across Underbarrow Pool to the marshy pastures below on Helsington Moss. However, there is no doubt that Brigsteer is 'the steer bridge' inverted.

Brigsteer is also mentioned on a document of 1315 in which

there is a wrangle over some pasture-land between Sir Walter de Strickland and Sir Matthew de Redman. Today, the only 'wrangle' between the two great houses, Sizergh Castle and Levens Hall, might be over the number of tourists each is able to lure during the season! To put the document in somewhat light contemporary terms:

> Tourists who visit Sizergh Castle may also be allowed to visit Levens Hall at all times of the year 'outside the old hedges justly raised' after the ice-creams, the hot-dogs and the candy floss have been duly eaten; but that if any should linger in the grounds of Levens intent on eating more ice-creams, hot-dogs and candy floss, the grim Lord of Sizergh and his heirs may lawfully enter and grab the tourists by the scruff of the neck and drag them back to Sizergh to eat even more ice-creams, hot-dogs and candy floss.

Fortunately such a hideous picture is sheer fantasy, for 'both your houses' are bastions of dignity and decorum, and you would have to hunt hard for the bubble-gum beneath the bannisters. As both might say: 'There is nothing Bath or Bedford about us.'

Sizergh Castle

The pasture-land dispute between the Strickland, or Strikland, family and the Redmans brings us conveniently up to the front of the Strickland family home, Sizergh Castle, which now belongs to the National Trust. This magnificent house has developed from a fourteenth-century pele tower, the greater part being Elizabethan, with a central block and two large wings which form a three-sided courtyard.

The Stricklands came to Sizergh by marriage in 1239, when Sir William Strickland married Elizabeth Deincourt, who had inherited the property on the death of her brother. Elizabeth was the great-granddaughter of Gervase Deincourt, who had been granted Sizergh, together with estates in Lincolnshire, by Henry II. Sir William was fortunate in his marriage and the Stricklands settled at Sizergh having previously lived at Great Strickland, near Appleby, the family deriving its name from the place.

The Strickland's part in the history of Westmorland has been full and important; staunchly loyal to both church and state before the Reformation, after the break with Rome, the family suffered a similar fate to that of the Leyburnes through the harshness of the recusancy laws.

As early as the reign of Henry III the family was given permission to have a private chapel at their Great Strickland home. The Bishop of Carlisle had given permission, provided it did not 'injure the revenues of the mother church of Morland', and the private chapel in Sizergh Castle is still an important feature of the house.

Many members of the family served the county as Knight of the Shire and, in 1415, Sir Thomas Strickland distinguished himself in Henry V's French War and carried the banner of St George, the most important banner on the field, at Agincourt! The Stricklands were Yorkists during the Wars of the Roses, apart from one member of the family who 'marched with the red rose in his cap at the head of 290 men from various manors, half of whom were provided with horses and the other half without'. This was Walter Strickland, another Walter. On the accession of Edward IV he obtained a general pardon indemnifying him for any offences committed.

The Stricklands were royalists during the Civil War and Sir Thomas Strickland was made a baronet on the field at Edgehill in 1642, according to tradition, though I have not been able to substantiate this. During the reign of Charles II a Sir Thomas Strickland was Keeper of the Privy Purse to Queen Catherine of Braganza, and his second wife, Winifred Trentham, became a member of Queen Mary of Modena's household and was present at the birth of James Edward Stuart, the Prince of Wales, who would later be known as the 'Old Pretender'. The Stricklands' staunch loyalty to the Stuarts took them into exile with the royal family in 1688, and they remained in voluntary exile at the Palace of St Germain until Sir Thomas Strickland died in 1694. Lady Strickland, it is said, acted as governess to the young Prince and among the many interesting things to be seen at Sizergh from the time of their exile is a series of portraits of the Stuart family given to Lady Strickland by the Queen, Mary of Modena.

Sir Thomas's son, Walter, returned to England and from that time the family's descendants have continued to live at the castle, as they still do. In 1950, the Sizergh estate was donated to

the National Trust. Like Levens Hall, Sizergh Castle is very
well-worth visiting; in fact, to visit both in one day, seeing as
they are so close together, is probably the best plan!

It was at Sizergh, some time during the 1920s, that the mural,
now in Helsington Church, was painted by Marion de Sonaret.
The artist has painted a heavenly host of angels against a
landscape background of the Lyth Valley, and, it is said, she
used local girls as models. The fair angels all have the face of
Mary Benson, of The Hyning, and the dark angels, that of
Annie Willan, of Brigsteer.

St John's, Helsington, is approached down a private track, but
it is fairly easy to park, and, in fine weather, provides a very
good spot from which to look down on the valley. There are even
strategically placed seats on which to sit.

The road that leads down into Brigsteer from the direction of
Helsington Church passes by the Wheatsheaf Hotel and on
towards Underbarrow, about three miles further north. As the
name tells us, Underbarrow is 'under the hill' or, rather, beside
it, and it is situated on what was once a packhorse track between
Kendal and Ulverston. The road is windy and up and down, and
must have been in earlier days a fairly difficult one to use. It is,
perhaps, not so surprising that many inns on the route are called
the Punch Bowl, and at Underbarrow the sign shows a welcom-
ing lass holding her bowl ready! Many of the gardens here have
little orchards of damson trees, which are special feature of the
Lyth Valley, and those who like damson jam, cheese, jelly, or
best of all, pickle, will be able to purchase fruit in the early
autumn.

The manor of Underbarrow was held by the Leyburnes until
1715 when their estates were forfeited to the Crown because of
John Leyburne's siding with the Earl of Derwentwater in the
First Jacobite Rebellion. The Leyburnes, besides owing Skelsmergh Hall, had their chief home at Cunswick Hall, in Underbarrow, about two miles north-east of the village, and below the
west side of Cunswick Scar. Cunswick means the 'king's farm'
and the hall that was for so long the Leyburne home was built on
to an early pele tower, though the tower was pulled down in
1582 when the owner, James Leyburne, was imprisoned in the
New Fleet, in Manchester, for his recusancy. In the summer of

that year two judges, Gawdy and Clench, came on the Northern Circuit and sat at Appleby, where Leyburne was fined £100 levied on his estates at Smardale, near Kirkby Stephen. This made no difference to his resolve to worship as he chose according to his conscience, and he was by the Christmas of 1582 arrested and confined in Carlisle Castle, where he remained for several weeks before being taken to Manchester. It is said he was taken right past the gates of his house in Skelsmergh on the way south and forbidden permission to enter, but taken on to Kendal for the night. After a spell in Manchester, Leyburne was taken south to London and imprisoned in the Tower where he was interrogated, and denying the Queen's supremacy in ecclesiastical matters, he rashly accused the Queen of being an usurper. This was enough to condemn him and he was sent back up north, and after a further spell in the New Fleet he was transferred to Lancaster for trial at the Lenten Assizes. He was found guilty of treason and hanged, drawn and quartered in Lancaster on the 22nd of March, 1583.

The year before his death James Leyburne had made a generous gift to the town of Kendal, where the family had a town house. As it records in *The Boke of Recorde of Kirkbie Kendal*:

> Mr James Leyburne of his liberality, for the use of the town and those coming and resorting unto the same, did freely give and bestow all his clock, furnished with sounding bell of the same, from his manor house of Cunswick, over and besides some oak trees for setting the clock upon.

No doubt at the time Leyburne would have wished he could have put the clock back!

7

The Lower Kent

*The tide was dead out, and the sands lay desolate
under the heavy sky.*

Constance Holme

It will have been noticed that both Witherslack and Crosthwaite
were chapelries of parishes on the east side of the Kent Estuary,
and that there was considerable toing and froing across the
sands, which, in the winter especially, must have been a hazardous business. I intend now to look at the east and south of the
estuary and the villages situated south of Levens as far as
Blackstone Point, the western extent of the south bank of the
Kent where the river's channel, visible only at low tide, crosses
over towards Grange-over-Sands. I begin with Heversham.

Heversham
Like so many attractive villages Heversham is now bypassed,
but a little detour takes one into the main street which was
formerly the main road, the A6 Lancaster to Kendal road.
Heversham, 'Heahfrith's homestead', is some six miles south-
by-west of Kendal and only one and a quarter miles from
Milnthorpe. It has an interesting history, not only because of its
famous school but also because it would seem to have been an
important place in Anglian times, and there is mention of a
monastery there in the eighth century. This would probably
have been a small collection of wooden buildings with a simple
church, and possibly the Anglian cross-shaft, which is now one
of Heversham's treasures, was placed there by those early
monks. The Angles founded several monasteries in the North
and when St Cuthbert arrived in Carlisle in AD 685, he discovered a monastery there already.

124

The Heversham cross is placed securely in the church porch
and what is remaining of it would suggest that it was never as
fine as crosses at Bewcastle or Ruthwell, but the design depicts
animals and birds, grapes and scrolls.

Heversham was among the many gifts Ivo de Tailbois made to
St Mary's, York. He gave the church and the advowson, that is,
the right to appoint the priest, and a third of the manor lands.
The remaining part was kept in the barony and was part of the
grant made to Alexander de Windsore when he married Agnes,
the daughter of William de Lancaster I. The manor remained in
the de Windsore family until the end of the fourteenth century
when, after passing through various families, it was eventually
bought by James Bellingham, in 1597. Heversham thus became
part of the Levens Hall estate.

The de Windsores had also held Grayrigg and Morland, near
Appleby, besides Heversham, although their main interest
seems to have been there. In 1334, Alexander de Windsore, as
lord of two parts of the manor, was granted the right to hold a
weekly market. This took place in Milnthorpe every Wednes-
day, and the charter also granted that each year there would be
a fair to celebrate the Feast of St Peter and St Paul, that is, on
the 29th of June; this was to be a two-day celebration because
the charter mentions the Eve and the Feast, so things 'got going'
at Heversham on the 28th!

The very next year Alexander de Windsore appears in
another record in a rather different context. He was accused of
trespassing on the land of Henry Fitz-Hugh at 'Mikelton in
Teesdale'. It is such records that make the hours of going
through them worthwhile, and I found that the same Alexander,
in 1320, had incurred the wrath of Roger de Clifford who
complained: 'That Alexander de Windsore and others broke into
his park at Qwynnefell, and took away eggs of his sparrow-
hawks lately nesting there, whereby he lost the profit of his
aery.' This member of the de Windsore family seems to have
shown a singular disregard for the rights of property which
might be said to equal that of De Quincey's Westmorland
sheep!

There are no signs of any stonework before the twelfth century
in the present church at Heversham, and this is not surprising

because it was very badly damaged by fire in 1601, as a manuscript book kept in the church records:

> Whereas ill-fortuned through negligence of a careless workman, being a plumber, anno Christi, 1601, on Wednesday being the first day of July, the Parish Church of Heversham, in the County of Westmorland, was utterly consumed by fire, and all implements, ornaments, books, monuments, chests, organs, bells and all other things were perished.

This record is not strictly accurate if the fine fifteenth-century chest now in the church was there at the time. Heversham is worth visiting for this one item alone; it is the longest chest I can remember seeing, made of oak and bound with iron, and with four locks!

Besides the items listed the fire destroyed the north arcade of the church, which had to be rebuilt completely, but the south arcade, though showing signs of restoration, is mostly the original twelfth-century stonework with three fifteenth-century windows above in the clerestory. The restoration work was carried out swiftly, for by 1610 the church was said to be 'in as good estate as the same was before the ruinous decay'. However, the most distinctive feature of Heversham Church, which is dedicated to St Peter, is the fine west tower seen clearly from the main road. This was designed by our old friends, Paley and Austin, in 1878, when they carried out what was described as a 'thorough restoration'.

Heversham School

Heversham is best known for its famous school which in recent times has been constantly in the news because of attempts to amalgamate it with the school at Milnthorpe. Heversham is a particularly early foundation, though nothing like as old as Kendal or Sedbergh Schools, both founded in 1525. It came into being when, in 1613, Edward Wilson, a wealthy gentleman from Nether Levens, founded and endowed a school 'to increase, maintain and continue religion, good learning and discipline in the parish'. With these good intentions in mind the school set out to fulfil the hopes of its founder, who had also prepared the way for two scholars, of little or no means, to continue their education at each of the universities. These scholars were obviously to be drawn from the area, though, it seems, only one had necessarily to be prepared at Heversham. The colleges chosen were Queen's College, Oxford, as might be expected, and Trinity College, Cambridge.

Edward Wilson was also very generous to the poor of the parish, particularly those dwelling across the sands. About a year after he had endowed the school he bought Heversham Hall but allowed a relative to live in it, preferring Nether Levens for himself, although he only rented the hall there. When he died in 1653, the family seem to have objected to the amount of money donated to charity and even tried to withhold the exhibitions he had set up at the school. The matter eventually went to court, at Lancaster, where the founder's will was upheld. All the details of the school's foundation are given in a book I much enjoyed reading: *Heversham: The Story of a Westmorland School and Village* by Rober Humber.

While Rev. Thomas Watson was headmaster of the school, Heversham turned out several pupils who were to achieve fame later as bishops, scholars and lawyers. Watson had arrived in 1698 and remained at the school for almost forty years, during which time he taught Heversham's most famous pupil, Ephraim Chambers, the author of *Cyclopaedia.*

Chambers had been born in 1680, the son of Richard Chambers, a small-time farmer from Milton, near Heversham. Ephraim was one of three brothers and, according to Cornelius Nicholson, he attended both Heversham and Kendal Schools. Mr Humber makes no mention of Kendal, and I am inclined to accept that Chambers received all his schooling at Heversham.

When he left school Chambers went up to London where he was apprenticed to a geographer and globe-maker called Senex. It is not known exactly how long Chambers remained with the globe-maker, and he may have completed his apprenticeship before moving to Gray's Inn to follow a career as a journalist, an occupation from which he seems to have been able to scrape up some kind of an income, writing anything for anyone who would pay him. It must have been at about this time that he decided to produce something even more spectacular than John Harris's *Lexicon Technicum* which had appeared in 1704.

In 1738, the two volumes of *Cyclopaedia, or an Universal*

Dictionary of Arts and Sciences were published by subscription at four guineas a time. The importance of Chambers's achievement was recognized immediately and the author of *Cyclopaedia* was made a member of the Royal Society in the following year. This was, no doubt, helped by the work being dedicated to George III, a shrewd move on Chambers's part.

Cyclopaedia was exceedingly well written and went into several editions. For the second edition of 1738 Chambers intended to add some further material but decided against it, later publishing his *Considerations* separately. The effect of Chambers' style on his readers was to have far-reaching results, for Dr Johnson told Boswell that he had formed his own style partly upon Chambers's proposal for his dictionary.

The French translation of *Cyclopaedia* became the forerunner of the equally famous *Encyclopédie* of Diderot and d'Alembert, and, indeed, Chambers's work was the precursor of all encyclopaedias to come. So famous was he when he died on the 15th of May, 1740, that he was buried in the cloisters of Westminster Abbey. After his death, two further editions of *Cyclopaedia* were published, in 1741 and 1746, but his name lives on even today and seems to be for ever linked with dictionaries, though, unlike the good Doctor Johnson who admitted his debt to Chambers, he never wrote a dictionary at all! The *Chambers Encyclopaedia* was nothing to do with Ephraim, but owed its origin to W. and R. Chambers, of Edinburgh, who started a publishing business and edited *Chambers Journal*. Their *Encyclopaedia* was begun in 1859 and completed in 1868. It was sheer coincidence that their name was the same as 'the father of all'!

Near the school is the site of the old cockpit, and it is known that Heversham, as well as other schools in the area, indulged in this gruesome sport. It was on Shrove Tuesday that the boys were allowed to bring their fighting-cocks to school. The rules of Kendal Grammar School, for instance, provided that the school was 'free to all the boys resident in the parish of Kendal, for classics alone, excepting a voluntary payment of a cock-penny'. The term 'cock-penny' did not mean literally a penny, but could be any sum stipulated by the master; this could vary according to the pupil's age and place in the school. At Heversham, the sum due varied between two shillings and twenty shillings, and it was considered a perfectly legitimate perk for the master,

The old Lancaster to Kendal Canal near Crooklands

being a valuable bonus to his income. At Sedbergh School each boy paid four and a half pence each year, ostensibly for the purchase of a fighting-cock for Shrove Tuesday. It is, perhaps, a reflection on our society that it is necessary to turn up at school with the latest 'hit' in the Record Charts in order to 'win one's spurs'!

Milnthorpe

Milnthorpe is a small market town situated about a mile due south of Heversham. For many centuries it was a township in Heversham Parish, becoming separated from it in 1838, the year after St Thomas's Church had been built in an attractive position east of the small market square. Except on Fridays, which is market day, it is possible to park a car in the square and take a walk around. The old market cross, a simple column with a ball finial, is set at the east end of the square.

Milnthorpe is 'the hamlet with a mill', an easy enough name to guess, but the use of the element 'thorpe' is not so common in Westmorland. It is an old East Scandinavian word which meant a secondary settlement, presumably in this case secondary to Heversham itself, the 'town' of the parish. There is a similar use of the word in Millthrop just outside Sedbergh, on the River Rawthay. Often, the fortification placed on a hill grew up as the main settlement, while the mill, such an important part of community life, would develop a small group of houses around it and the river. The mill, the 'miln' of Milnthorpe, was first mentioned in 1460. It was situated on the banks of the River Bela some way downstream from the perhaps grander mill at Beetham. However, there was to be far more activity at Milnthorpe than grinding corn for the community, for it was destined to become the only port in Westmorland!

Compared to the large ports on the West Cumberland coast, places like Whitehaven or Maryport, even, Milnthorpe was a very small port indeed. However, until the building of the viaduct across the Kent Estuary from Arnside to Sunnyside became necessary to carry the Carnforth to Ulverston section of the Furness Railway, the Kent was navigable as far as the mouth of the River Bela, and small ships could tie up at Milnthorpe. It seems most unlikely that there was anything amounting to a docks, but it is known that a certain amount of

A bridge over the Kent near Natland

coal was shipped into the port, as it was also into Grange, on the other side of the estuary, something which was to continue until the Lancaster to Kendal Canal was opened in 1819. It is a pity Milnthorpe could not have lingered on as a port until after the first photographs, for it is difficult to imagine the scene or to guess how large the vessels would have been. I suspect they would have been very small, perhaps weighing twenty tons or less.

On the north side of the village, Haverflatts Lane leads up towards Milnthorpe School and passes the small Catholic church of Christ the King. This fine modern building, built mostly of local stone, with a Langdale slate floor and an altar of polished Broughton slate, was consecrated in November 1970, and is a testimony to the craftsmen who built it. Milnthorpe should also be proud to possess such a magnificent example of contemporary ceramic sculpture as the *Way of the Cross* by the Polish artist, Adam Kossowski, which is inside the church. The ceramic is some twenty-nine feet long and depicts the fourteen Stations of the Cross, with the many figures set out in relief in glazed ceramic on an unglazed background. I would lay claim for this inspired piece to be the finest example of contemporary work in the county, but I have been exceedingly fortunate to have come across Kossowski's work elsewhere, particularly at Leyland, where there is a *Last Judgment* set above the entrance to the Benedictine priory church; and at Aylesford, in Kent, where Kossowski has decorated several chapels at the Carmelite friary, including in the Relic Chapel the magnificently black-and-gold reliquary of St Simon Stock, the founder of the English Carmelites; and the beautiful 'red' Chapel of the English Martyrs. At Aylesford Kossowski was working on a much grander scale, and his *Stations of the Cross* there are fourteen separate pieces: at Milnthorpe, where the wall space at his disposal was so much less, he wisely decided on one large piece in which the eye may follow the inevitable drama of the Crucifixion. However, there are two further small ceramics by the same artist at the church: the figure of *Christ the King* on the outside of the building by the main door; and *Our Lady and the Infant Jesus* above the Lady Altar. Also inside, and an important feature of the church, is the stained-glass window designed and made by the monks of Buckfast Abbey.

Constance Holme

The novelist Constance Holme was born at Milnthorpe on the 7th of October, 1880. She was the daughter of John Holme and his wife, Elizabeth Cartmel, and the family lived at Owlet Ash above the village. Constance was the youngest of fourteen children and she attended a school at Arnside before being sent away, first to Birkenhead, then later to Blackheath. We must accept her word for it that she was a lonely child, but at an early age she revealed her gift for story-telling with which she used to entertain her school friends. However, nothing meant more to her than the area of her home, from which she was to draw almost all the imagery for her novels.

Constance Holme's father was agent to the Dallam Tower estate, so the family was relatively well-off and Constance remained at Milnthorpe during the early years of her adult life until she left home to marry Frederick Punchard, the agent for the Underley Hall estate of Lord Bentinck, in 1916. It was at home, then, that her first novel *Crump Folk Going Home* was written. This was published in 1913, and was followed a year later by what is probably her finest book *The Lonely Plough*.

The popularity of *The Lonely Plough* was slow in growing, and it was not until some twenty years after the book first appeared that one bookseller in Leeds sold some 2,500 copies in a year! This tender book relates the lives of those living on a great landed estate, 'an ancient system working at its best', and was partly inspired by a freak storm which brought exceptionally high tides and terrible flooding to the area, in 1907. That year the tidal bore, which usually runs itself out at Arnside, came sweeping over the land and flooded several houses in the Sandside area:

> Slowly the wreck of things was pulled back into symmetry and order, houses carpeted and papered, Dutch barns rebuilt, fences set up again, the mutilated roads laid and rolled. The Let, too, had had all its yawning mouths filled and strengthened, and the dykes and cuts were deepened and increased. So the patched marsh grew trim again, and by the time the haycutter sang on the hill, the land below

had gathered itself out of the horrors of destruction into a growing likeness of its old beauty.

Constance Holme was the only twentieth-century novelist to have all her novels published in the 'World's Classics' series. This was because Sir Humphrey Milford, the chairman of the Oxford University Press, admired her work; but for the most part, it was an honour deserved.

Constance Holme's third novel, published in the year of her marriage, was *The Old Road from Spain*, in which she drew from incidents real and imaginary in the lives of her mother's ancestors, particularly the legend, which I suppose is quite plausible, 'to the effect that an Armada vessel, wrecked in Morecambe Bay, cast up a waif (or waifs) on a certain fell, from which the family took its name'. Constance Holme claimed similar, though even earlier, traditions for her father's family, which could trace itself back to John of Stockholm, the Viking who sailed up the Tyne in 780! Perhaps it is that land agents, who spend their lives managing the affairs of those with illustrious ancestries, feel more secure with wild pasts of their own!

In 1919, and now living at Kirkby Lonsdale, Constance Holme wrote her fourth novel *The Splendid Fairing*. This came out a year later and, in 1920, won for its author the Prix Femina Vie Heureuse, the French literary award, which another novelist with whom Constance Holme is often compared, Mary Webb, was to receive in 1924 for *Precious Bain*.

Other novels were to follow: *Beautiful End*; *The Trumpet in the Dust*; and the tale of a gardener, *The Things Which Belong*. These post-war novels show an increased awareness of human suffering and the nobility of endurance. Although these books received good reviews none of them sold very well, and the last years of Constance Holme's life were sad on this account. In 1930 *He-Who Came?* was published, which was her last novel to be so, but after the author's death the typescript of the almost completed 'The Jasper Sea' was discovered among her papers.

When Mr Punchard retired from Underley Hall, he was happy to live in the old family home in Milnthorpe in which his wife had spent her early life, and, although the marriage was successful in a quiet way only, Constance Holme was deeply distressed when her husband died in 1946. She remained in

Milnthorpe for eight more years before moving to Arnside shortly before she herself died, in the June of 1955, although the funeral was held in St Thomas's Church, Milnthorpe.

Out of Constance Holme's eight published novels, it seems to me that *The Splendid Fairing* and *The Lonely Plough* are of special merit, but I have always hated having to judge other people's work, and I am no critic!

'It's always one man's hand on the lonely plough'.

Beetham

Beetham is situated south of Heversham and Milnthorpe, but, as I have mentioned already, it was once a very large parish with extensive land over the sands including Meathop, Ulpha, and Witherslack within its bounds. The two townships south of the Kent Estuary were Farleton and Haverbrack and, what is today known as Beetham was, in fact, Haverbrack, 'the slope where oats were grown', a name now restricted to a much smaller area a little further north.

Beetham appears in Domesday Book as 'Biedun', and the name is spelt in several different ways in early records. It is thought that the origin of the place-name, and that of the River Bela, is the same Old Norse word for an embankment, so that Beetham means something like 'among the embankments': presumably this is a reference to early efforts made to control the flooding of the Bela and the direction of the river's course.

Domesday Book lists Beetham among the manors held by Tostig, so it would have later become part of Roger de Poitou's holding. However, it is not long before a family using the name of the place appears in records, and a Thomas de Betham had been Knight of the Shire for Westmorland several times before his death, in 1314. It was the same Thomas who had been granted a charter by Edward II, in 1311, to hold a weekly market in Beetham, but there is no market there today, and neither is there need of it with the village being so near Milnthorpe.

After holding the manor for some two hundred years, the de Bethams were deprived of the land for supporting the Yorkist cause in the Wars of the Roses, and Beetham became part of the vast grant of land with which Henry VII rewarded the Stanleys for their part in the Battle of Bosworth. The home of the de

Bethams had been situated south of the Bela, and some of the original stonework may still be seen among the complex of farm buildings at Beetham Hall, though most of the old part is in ruins. The hall is a familiar sight to anyone travelling along the A6 towards Kendal from the Carnforth direction, and part of the curtain wall of the fourteenth-century, fortified manor house is still standing, but the present farmhouse is of a much later date, having been built in the seventeenth century, In 1644, the Parliamentarian army besieged the hall and the tradition is that they also entered Beetham Church with a mob, including some locals, broke up the stained-glass windows and knocked off the heads of the effigies of Sir Thomas de Betham and his wife. Whether this is true or not Beetham Church is one of the most historically interesting churches in the area, with its ninth-century tower-base and twelfth-century south arcade. Unlike so many Westmorland churches Beetham gives the impression of age, though one of the features that caught my eye is not so old. This was a window in the west end of the nave of 1859 which has stained-glass lights showing in the centre St Ethelburga, who is not unusual in northern churches because she married King Edwin of Northumbria! However, the two saints on either side of her, St Lioba and St Osyth, are unusual for the north, and, indeed, are fairly unusual anywhere. St Lioba had worked as a missionary with St Boniface in Germany in the eighth century, and was Abbess of Bischofsheim after moving from Wimborne, in Dorset; and St Osyth was an Anglo-Saxon princess who was martyred after founding the Abbey of Chich, in Essex. I noticed that the information card by the window identified St Osyth with St Sitha, this is a very common error and needs correcting: St Sitha or Zita, who gives her name to Sith Lane, in London, was an Italian girl from Lucca, who died in 1272. Why are these three unlikely saints at Beetham? The answer is probably that there were chantry chapels to all three in the church before the Reformation, and there are marks in the stonework to show us where the wooden screens were set into the walls. What fun Cromwell's lads would have had with those!

Dallam Tower
Almost a mile west of the village, and set in its own magnificent park, is the home of the Wilson family, Dallam Tower. This

impressive house was built in 1720 or, at least, Daniel Wilson put the work in hand in that year. It would have taken some time to complete. Dallam was built on the site of an earlier house and takes its name from a family that held land at Haverbrack. A Robert Dalam, with one 'l', is recorded as holding part of the manor, in 1522, and there is a gateway into the kitchen-garden bearing the date 1683, which is about all that remains of any earlier dwelling today.

Dallam was elaborated in about 1826, when the side pavilions and the large porch of four Tuscan columns were added. All is on a fairly small scale compared with similar estates in the South of England, and one feels that had Alexander Pope seen it he would probably have left it alone, for it hardly comes up to 'Timon's Villa' in grandeur, or even lack of taste. There was nothing about the Wilson family that might have roused Pope into action, as did the Duke of Chandos and his estate, Canons!

However, Dallam Tower must have turned a few local eyes in its heyday with its deer park and its newly planted beeches, many of which have had to come down recently in their old age. Also the park was renowned for its rookery and its heronry; and there is an account of a battle between the rooks and herons that took place in 1775, when the larger birds decided to take over some of the rooks' territory. In 1877, Thomas Gough, of Arnbarrow, reported twenty-seven herons' nests at Dallam in his *Observations of the Heron and Heronry at Dallam Tower*.

Arnside

If anyone is interested in bird-watching, then Arnside is a good place to see the hundreds of waders that either inhabit Morecambe Bay, or visit it in the winter. There is also the wide area, controlled by the Royal Society for the Protection of Birds, not so far away at Leighton Moss. Leighton Moss is outside the confines I have set myself, but it is famous for the bitterns that breed there, and the ospreys, which are now, thanks to the society's work, not quite so rare as they were.

Arnside has the 'look' of a seaside resort at the beginning of the century, but it is not so very long ago that this small township in Beetham Parish was a small line of fishermen's houses, and an insignificant place. Arnside owes its development to the railway and, like Grange-over-Sands, it was the building of the Furness Railway in the 1850s that started it all. The railway was originally called the Ulverston and Lancaster Railway, and it required a viaduct across the narrowest part of the Kent Estuary. It was a strange coincidence that the length of the viaduct was exactly the same distance, 522 feet, as the height of Arnside Knott, the wooded hill that dominates the little town.

Work began on the viaduct in the autumn of 1856 and continued until the July of the following year. The engineer, James Brunless, decided to sink hollow piles, about thirty feet in length, into the sand; these would stand on cast-iron discs six feet in diameter, so that the piles would not sink further. Such a measure was necessary because when the preliminary excavations were made it was discovered that the nearest firm rock was some ninety feet below the surface! Brunless's method worked, although it has been considerably reinforced since.

Arnside was separated from Beetham in 1870, when it became a parish in its own right with a fine church in the early Gothic style, St James's, designed by the Kendal architect, Miles Thompson, who had earlier been responsible for St Paul's, Ireton, in Wasdale. With the expanding population at Arnside St James's had to be enlarged in 1905, and again at the outbreak of the First World War.

Arnside is 'Arnulf's headland', taking its name from some early settler. The 'headland' is Arnside Knott; a *knot* being the Old Norse word for a hillock, or rocky hill. Today, the Knott and the surrounding woodland belongs to the National Trust, so it is saved from the fate of so much around it which has been mercilessly developed. The eastern side, towards Hagg Wood, has become a sprawling series of rows of houses.

To the south of the Knott there is a ruined pele tower, built in 1375. This must have been an important defensive position, and the very last in the line of such towers situated along the south bank of the Kent Estuary. Arnside Tower was destroyed by fire at the end of Elizabeth I's reign, as the Lancaster Parish Register records: 'The 27th day of October at night being in the year of Our Lord God 1602. Being a mighty wind was Arnside Tower burned, as it pleased God to permit.' It is difficult to assess to what extent the tower was rebuilt after this catastrophe, but it had been bringing in no income since 1517! The ruin, which is

situated on the outskirts of Middlebarrow Wood and is easily
seen from the road, shows that at one time there were four
storeys, but most of the west wall and the interior partition were
blown down in a fierce gale, in 1884.

If anyone wishes to play the part of Childe Roland and come to
the 'dark tower', it would be difficult to choose which to come to,
since there is another, Hazelslack Tower, about two miles to the
north-east. On the day for me Childe Harold to the dark tower
came, he nearly broke his neck on the 'fairy steps', but lived to
tell the tale!

8

Cartmel over Sands

I can advise no stranger to go this way.
John Wesley

At one time Cartmel was approached more often than not by coach across the sands from Hest Bank, some three miles north of Lancaster, to Kent's Bank, a convenient spot two miles north of Humphrey Head Point, the most southerly tip of the Cartmel Peninsula. A traveller remembering the experience of crossing the sands in about 1830 recalled:

> The large coach swayed from side to side wending its way across the stretch of sands. Sometimes the horses plunged into the channel, a proceeding that appeared to drift us away out to the distant line of the sea; but after much whipping and splashing we were safe out of the water and landed on the sand again.

It sounds alarming, but the coachman would have been experienced, and a guide would have been on hand to lead the way through the channels and quicksands. The channels were those of the River Keer which flows into the bay, near Carnforth, and the Kent which follows the curve of the coastline from Grange-over-Sands to Humphrey Head. The distance of the route from Hest Bank to Kent's Bank was about seven miles, and the course taken arched round by Warton Sands in a northerly direction till, opposite Jenny Brown's Point, it turned more sharply eastward. In considering the sands-crossing it is always important to remind oneself that the whole of Morecambe Bay would be washed over by the tide twice in every twenty-four hours, so that although a traveller whose destination was Cartmel might feel a sense of arrival on reaching Kent's Bank, those who had

138

further to go, to Ulverston, say, or Furness, would only consider it as part of the way. They would be unable to make the next leg of the journey, the crossing over Leven Sands, sometimes known as Cartmel Sands, for another twelve hours! This waiting for the tide was a boon to the various innkeepers who kept hostelries along the route, and in Flookburgh particularly there were many inns. The more important travellers, perhaps, made their way to the priory, for this was, and still is, the centre of Cartmel.

The local people seem to have been up to all kinds of tricks to delay the travellers for as long as possible and so benefit the more from their trade. This was something that John Wesley noticed when he made the crossing in the May of 1759:

> I have taken leave of the sand road. I believe it is ten measured miles shorter than the other, but there are four sands to pass so far from each other that it is scarcely possible to pass them all in one day, especially as you have all the way to do with a generation of liars who detain all travellers as long as they can, for their own gain as their neighbours. I can advise no stranger to go this way.

The alternative route overland, Wesley mentions, was the way via Kendal, Ambleside, and Keswick, eventually reaching Whitehaven by way of Lorton and Cockermouth. Also, it will have been noticed that Wesley refers to 'four sands to pass', and he means, besides the two I have mentioned already, the Dudden and Ravenglass Sands, though the last was a very short crossing compared with the other three.

The Parish of Cartmel was cared for by the priory until the Reformation. Originally there were three townships: Holker, Allithwaite and Broughton, but later these were divided further so that there were eight townships in all: Cartmel Town, Upper and Lower Allithwaite, Broughton, Staveley, Cartmel Fell, and Upper and Lower Holker. Broughton would be known as Broughton East in order to differentiate it from Broughton in Furness; and Staveley was known as Staveley in Cartmel, so that it would not be confused with the other Staveley on the upper reaches of the River Kent. Cartmel is almost completely surrounded by water except for the northern tip; by the shores of Windermere, the Rivers Leven and Winster, and then, of course, the sea. The River Winster, as we have seen, marked the old

boundary between Westmorland and Lancashire north of the
sands, but it was also the eastern boundary of Cartmel, and
Cartmel was very much part of Lancashire until the creation of
Cumbria, in 1974.

Cartmel Priory
The Augustinian canons settled in Cartmel in 1188 when Wil-
liam Marshall, Lord of Cartmel, founded the priory.
Marshall was described at the time as 'the foremost man in
England', and he was created Earl of Pembroke by King John.
In the Priory Charter the founder states that:

> This house have I founded for the increase of Holy Religion, giving
> and conceding to it every kind of liberty that mouth can utter or the
> heart of man can conceive; whosoever therefore shall cause loss or
> injury to the said house or its inmates may he incur the curse of God
> and of the Blessed Virgin Mary and of all the other saints of God,
> besides my particular malediction.

It was for the last phrase that I included the whole sentence!
Marshall had endowed the priory with land, not only with
estates close at hand but in Ireland also, and, as a particular
favourite of Henry II, his estates were vast. The canons, known
as Canons Regular because they followed a 'regula', or rule of
discipline, were followers of St Augustine, the Bishop of Hippo
in North Africa, and not to be confused with St Augustine of
Canterbury. When they came to Cartmel they found a church
already in existence and dedicated it to St Michael the
Archangel; but finding this unsuitable for their purpose they
demolished it and built their priory church on the same site. The
new church was dedicated to the Blessed Virgin Mary, though
St Michael had a special altar dedicated to him for the use of
parishioners, and it was the fact that the priory was used also as
a parish church that would save it when the monastery was
dissolved, in 1536.

Much of what may be seen today at Cartmel Priory is original,
especially the chancel, the transepts and the main doorway;
these are not strictly speaking Norman, but what is known
as Transitional, from a few years before Early English architectural work began. However, the church might have taken

many years to complete, and there are good reasons to believe that the work was still in progress in 1230. Anyhow the priory was anxious about money, and the Archbishop of York issued a special indulgence of 20 days to all who gave their goods towards the fabric of the church of St Mary of Cartmel. This desperate remedy was blessed by Pope Gregory IX who, in 1233, sent word to 'his beloved children, the Prior and monks, to inform them he had taken their church under his protection'.

One of the sadnesses of so many great churches is that very little of the mediaeval glass remains. This was not caused principally by the Reformation but by the iconoclastic enthusiasm of the Commonwealth times. We have already seen how the glass at Beetham was smashed up in 1644. At Cartmel there was once a magnificent east window, which had been positioned in 1410; what remains today to be seen is largely through the energies of the parishioners. The three lights were restored in 1964 and they show the Virgin and Child, John the Baptist, and the Archbishop, William of York. Cartmel would be worth visiting for these alone, but the woodwork of the priory must take pride of place, much of which was carved in the middle of the fifteenth century. The oak stalls and misericords are of that date, but there is much later seventeenth-century work of Flemish origin, particularly the screen and the canopies which were erected over the stalls in 1620 as a gift from George Preston, of Holker Hall.

The misericords carved beneath the lifting-seats in the choir are a common feature of religious houses where the community would have spent several hours during the course of each day in prayer. Such seats gave rest to the feet, since a monk was able to half sit whilst giving the impression of standing! As the name implies it showed some mercy, for the Latin *misericordia* means 'compassion' or 'pity'. The men who carved the misericords at Cartmel were considerable craftsmen, yet their names will never be known, and their work largely hidden. It is as though they say to us: 'We give you a symbol, a sign. What looks plain and ordinary is not when you look more closely. Consider these stalls made of dull wood, yet every one when examined will reveal its own treasure.' On the hidden treasures at Cartmel the carvers let rip! There were originally twenty-six misericords in all and only one is now missing; here, Alexander the Great, a peacock, an elephant, an ape and many other birds, animals and flowers are used to represent deeper mysteries; for every carving instructs, as we see in the third seat on the south side, for instance, where the pelican feeding her young, it was once thought, from her own flesh and blood, is a symbol of Christ who gave his body and blood for the sins of many.

There is very much more that could be said about the priory and it is fortunate, therefore, that Professor J. C. Dickinson's *The Land of Cartmel* is still in print for anyone who wishes to know more, unlike another excellent book *Cartmel: People and Priory* by Sam. Taylor.

Cartmel is a most attractive place to walk around, and there are many other things of interest such as the Priory Gatehouse or Peter Bain Smith's Bookshop, or, if one were wanting railroadiana, the famous bookshop of Norman Kerr, the brother of Ewen Kerr who runs the equally fine shop in Kendal. Around the Market Square there are craft-shops and tea-shops, and an art gallery opposite the priory. On Whit Monday the Cartmel Races are held in the park and there is never a greater throng than on that day! It was in the park too that the cock-fighting 'mains' were once fought, and where the eggs laid by the wives of some of these 'conquerors', having been brightly decorated by the children, were rolled in the Easter pace-egging contests. During Holy Week the children had dyed or painted the hard-boiled eggs and taken them to show the folk who had donated them:

> Here's two or three Jolly Boys all in one mind.
> We've come a Pace-egging, we hope you'll prove kind,
> We hope you'll prove kind with your eggs and strong beer
> And we'll come no more nigh you until the next year.
>   Foll-der-i-iddle-i-day.

Lower Allithwaite

Cartmel, 'the sandbank by rocky ground', is the name of a large area, as we have seen, and what is now known by that name was formerly called Church Town. However, the town was divided more or less into two by the little River Ea, which in the early days when Cartmel was divided into three townships was the boundary between Holker and Allithwaite, so that there existed the incongruous situation of the priory's gatehouse being in a different township from the priory itself! With the rearrangement into eight townships all became easier.

The two main hamlets in Lower Allithwaite are Allithwaite Village and Kent's Bank, which though once a small village is now 'swallowed up' by Grange-over-Sands. Kent's Bank would seem to have been the more lively village of the two being the point at which the coaches reached drier land after their trip across the sands. Here the Abbot of Furness had his own residence built upon land granted to the abbey in 1160 by Thomas, son of Gospatric, of Workington. Like the Abbot of York's house in Kendal, it was known as Abbot Hall, and would have provided rest and shelter for the Furness party while they waited for the next tide. The abbot of an important monastery like Furness would of necessity be away for much of the time visiting the many estates held by the abbey, or other monasteries. It is thought, for instance, that Swineshead Abbey, in Lincolnshire, was founded from Furness, and such ventures would have required much planning and necessitated travelling long distances. The Abbots of Furness must have been familiar with the sands, unlike the Priors of Cartmel, for William Marshal had laid it down that Cartmel was never to be raised to the status of an abbey!

The name Kirkhead or Kirkett given to a hill above Abbot Hall may mean that the monks had a small chapel there, but nothing remains of the monastic dwellings which after the Dissolution became a private house. Today, there is a large house on the site in use as a Methodist Guild Holiday Home: a sign on the roadside announces 'Abbot Hall' with the motto 'One Heart, One Way'; but there are other reminders that this was once monastic land, for Priory Road, Priory Crescent, Abbot's Way and Abbot's Close are all nearby: row upon row of small bungalows hugging the hillside and most allowing their occupants a glimpse of sea and sand. Perhaps these pastel-shaded boxes stand upon land that once supported, if not fattened, the five cows kept to supply the Abbot's party with milk, butter and cheese; all part of what is truly called Christian Endeavour, whose Holiday Home is right opposite the station!

At Kent's Bank Station the road turns sharply northwards towards Allithwaite, 'the thwaite, or clearing, of Eilifr'. Those Norsemen get in everywhere it seems but perhaps not, for I have seen it also suggested that the name owes its origin to the Holy Well situated by Humphrey Head. However, to investigate further we will have to pass through Allithwaite which is a built-up, sprawling village along the Cartmel road.

Humphrey Head

It is fairly difficult to reach Humphrey Head by road, and almost impossible to park a car by the roadside once one has arrived. The way down on to the sands over a cattle-grid is messy and I would not advise it, even if one were foolhardy enough to park on the sands! The first part of the way from Allithwaite, however, is relatively easy and takes one past Wraysholme Tower which is worth pausing by to inspect.

Wraysholme, often spelt Raisholm, was held by the Harrington family whose main residence was Gleaston Castle, in Low Furness, and who, it may be remembered, held the tower at Yewbarrow, in Longsleddale. It seems likely that Wraysholme provided shelter for the Harringtons in much the same way as Abbot Hall when members of the family wished to cross the sands, besides being a useful defensive position and easily manned in times of trouble. This is the only example of a pele tower in Cartmel, and today, the tower is part of the farm outbuildings. When the Harrington line eventually died out, Wraysholme was part of the Lancashire estates given to the Stanleys, although it seems unlikely that that family ever lived there, preferring to lease it out; and it is known a family named Dicconson, or Dickinson, held it at one time.

At low tide it is possible to walk round Humphrey Head Point, though it is important to keep a constant watch as tides come up exceedingly fast. However, if the times of the tides are checked it is perfectly safe. Climbing up the cliff from the bottom, on the other hand, is probably not. There is a stone with the inscription:

> Beware how you these rocks ascend
> Here William Pedder met his end.

Hutton Roof and Ingleborough

The accident took place on the 22nd of August 1857, and little William Pedder was only 10 years old. Better not attempt the rocks at all.

Humphrey Head is about 160 feet high, though it seems higher from the sands. On the western side, that is the road side, is a spring. Marked on the map as Holy Well Spa, this was celebrated at one time for its medicinal qualities. It is recorded in a small book *Sketches of Grange*, published in Kendal, in 1850, from articles that appeared first in the literary corner of the *Kendal Mercury*, that the spa was frequented by miners from Alston. These presumably were lead miners, who rode all the way on their little mountain 'Galloways' and put themselves up in the neighbouring villages. The author says the miners bathed and drank the spa waters in quantity, 'a gallon per diem sometimes', and went back renewed and invigorated. Some returned annually for forty years, perhaps to visit again and again the small cottage situated near the well, though I could find no trace of it whatsoever. It was there that Old Rachel, a fisherman's wife, 'her dishevelled locks floating over her disordered attire', dispensed her potions to twenty or thirty horsemen crowding round her dirty door. When she was not handing out her medicines she would tell stories holding a short pipe 'black with forty years' usage, and which she smoked vehemently at every short interval of her tale'.

Up on the cliff top above the well there is a cave, known locally as the Fairy Cave in which, according to tradition, a wolf was trapped and killed. Some said it was the last wolf to be killed in England, but there is no way of telling; however a poem 'The Last Wolf' written in the late nineteenth century accepts the tradition as fact. This may be use of poetic licence, but the tale is not impossible.

Holker

Lower Holker is situated west of Lower Allithwaite and a road leads from Allithwaite village to Flookburgh, which at one time was a market town of some importance, having been granted a charter by Edward I which was later confirmed by Henry IV, and Charles II, in 1665.

There seems to be some confusion as to the origin of the name; some scholars claiming that the name is 'Floki's burgh', where

St Gregory's, Preston Patrick
Killington Reservoir at sunset

Floki is the name of some Norse chief who owned the place at one time. But just as often it is said to be 'Flooc burgh' from the Old English *Flooc*, meaning a flook or plaice. The latter seems more likely. At one time the land south of the village, now so successfully drained by dykes and an embankment, would have been more sand, and it is said there were times of exceptionally high tides when the sea washed over the streets. Today, the sea is about a mile away, and on this reclaimed land cattle are grazing near a small airfield and the campus of the Lakeland Caravan Centre.

Flookburgh has what looks like a market square, but this is in fact the site of the old chapel and graveyard. The market cross is standing in a second much smaller square opposite the Hope and Anchor Inn; I say square but, with the construction of a wider, modern road which breaks the square, it is necessary to imagine what it might have looked like. Further down the street, eastwards on the south side there is a small row of cottages built in 1665, while a little further still the Manor House announces that it was built in 1686. These dates are significant for it is thought that Flookburgh was devastated by the plague at about the same time as the Great Plague in London, and in 1686 there was a terrible fire in which some twenty-two houses were burnt, together with their outbuildings and barns. In the plague epidemic so many people died that they were buried in Eccleston Meadow in common graves and not in the consecrated ground of the graveyard, at Cartmel, so that with the fire afflicting an already diminished population it is doubtful whether the place was rebuilt fully. Anyway, it seems the Manor House dates from that time and the cost for rebuilding some houses in Flookburgh was met by public subscription after a petition had been lodged with the Crown.

Almost opposite the Manor House there is another inn, the Crown Inn, which like the Hope and Anchor is painted white with duck-egg blue window-frames and trimmings. It livens the place up a little, but I could not help wishing Flookburgh was still on the sea and that I could have witnessed the activity on the beach, yet it is still a 'fishing' village for all that.

Flookburgh Parish Church, a few hundred yards up the Cark road, is an impressively large building, erected in 1900 in a type of Early English style by local builders, Blairs of Allithwaite, from plans drawn up by Paley and Austin, the cost of which was almost entirely met by the Cavendish family. This church, dedicated to St John the Baptist, replaced the earlier chapel which stood in the centre of the village. It is thought that a chapel had stood on that site since the thirteenth century, and it would have been served by the Canons of Cartmel or a priest appointed by them. After the Dissolution Flookburgh seems to have been seriously neglected; in 1650 it is recorded that there was no minister or endowment, and by 1723 there was no table or font, or any surplice for the preacher. Then some fifty years later the old chapel was pulled down, not without difficulty for the walls were so thick, and a new chapel built that served the people until the new church was built. Today, this houses among other things the charter granted to the Borough of Flookburgh to hold a weekly market by Charles II.

Barely a mile south-west of Flookburgh is a crescent of houses once known as Flookburgh West but now Ravenstown, taking its name from a farmstead Raven Winder, which lies about a mile and a half further south. When one sees Ravenstown on the map it looks odd enough, but a visit confirms the opinion and something made me think of the war before I knew anything about the place. These houses in Ravenstown, though now mostly in private hands, were intended to lodge the personnel and staff of a naval aerodrome towards the end of the First World War, but the scheme was abandoned. The houses, tall, semi-detached dwellings with roofing, red-tiled or slate alternately, were again used during the Second World War until they were purchased by Vickers and used to house staff from the Barrow shipyards. With a good train service it was a practical scheme.

The two farms, Raven Winder and Canon Winder, though I notice the Ordnance Survey map has it 'Cannon Winder', are very ancient and are both part of the Holker Estate. Of the two only Canon Winder remains architecturally interesting, chiefly for its wide circular chimney at the back.

Cark
From Flookburgh the road leads northwards towards Cark, a small village which takes its name from a Celtic word meaning

a rock. At one time this was known as Nether Cark, in order to distinguish it from High Cark, which was situated further north in the Staveley township of Cartmel, and it is here that the second railway station on the peninsula is situated: Cark and Cartmel, the next stop after Kent's Bank, if one were travelling westward.

The close proximities of Flookburgh, Cark and Holker Hall has always been somewhat puzzling to strangers, and when a new incumbent arrived to take over St John's, at Flookburgh, the churchwarden told him: 'It's a bit muddling at first for them as doesn't know . . . t' girt house is at Holker, the cattle market and station are at Cark, and t' Church is at Flookburgh. They're all yan place, so to say, but very different from yan another, as ye'll find.' Canon Sam. Taylor who tells that story also speaks of the hostility between the two communities of Cark and Flookburgh, places less than two miles apart!

Cark Hall was at one time the property of the Pickering family, though it passed by marriage to the Curwens, in 1606, and later still to the Rawlinsons. This late Elizabethan or early Jacobean house is in its way very much more attractive than the other hall, at Holker!

When I spoke of Paley and Austin designing the church at Flookburgh I was putting the cart before the horse, perhaps I should say putting the Cartmel before the horse, for Holker Hall is what Nikolaus Pevsner called their 'outstanding domestic work'. The old hall had been damaged by a terrific fire that broke out on the 9th of March, 1871. In this the whole of the west wing was destroyed taking with it many priceless treasures in the way of paintings and furniture. The 7th Duke of Devonshire was staying in the house at the time, and it was he who employed the Lancaster firm to design the new hall, a very much grander affair than the house they designed for the Wakefields at Sedgwick!

Holker, pronounced 'Hooker', had been the home of the Preston family since the sixteenth century, and we have seen how George Preston was so generous to the Priory. It was George Preston's grandson, Thomas Preston, who, dying with no son to inherit the estate, passed it to his daughter, Catherine, wife of Sir William Lowther. The grandson of these two, another Sir

William Lowther, remained unmarried, and left the estate to his cousin, Lord George Augustus Cavendish, the second son of the 3rd Duke of Devonshire, which is how the Cavendishes, the present owners, came to own Holker.

Holker must be visited, not only for its fine interior but for its beautiful garden. One of the treasures of the place is the embroidered screen worked by Mary, Queen of Scots, but there are many interesting pictures, among which I noticed a self-portrait by Van Dyck and a painting of Thomas Fairfax, the Parliamentarian commander in the Civil War, besides one of Charles II!

Grange-over-Sands

Grange owes its reputation and popularity to the railway, and like the smaller resort of Arnside on the southern side of the estuary, Grange was virtually unknown until the Furness Railway was opened in 1857. Crossing the Kent at the narrowest point between Arnside and the marshes of Meathop, the railway followed the coastline on a specially constructed embankment to Kent's Bank. In doing so it would always mean that the track would come between the town of Grange and the shore, so that one has constantly to look over the railway to take in the view!

The chief advantage of Grange as a resort was that it faced south and was well sheltered from the north-westerly, north and north-easterly winds; while it benefited to some extent from the warm currents of the Gulf Stream. It was because of the similarity between the climate here and some of the resorts on the south-west coast that Grange was nicknamed the 'Torquay of the North' and became such a popular wintering place. As one of the many guidebooks says: 'The claim that Grange is advantageous for invalids has been so fully recognised by the highest medical authorities that it needs no further attestation.' Need I say more than that?

The name of the place owes its origin to a farm once situated near the shore, once owned by the priory at Cartmel. There is still a Grange Marsh Farm marked on the map, but the original one is said to have stood more or less where the present Police Station stands, so it could be said that it is still the centre of operations!

As the farm was only part of the priory estates, there are precious few records to draw from. In 1598, Grange appears to have been a port, and twelve tons of 'sea coal' worth 4s. 8d. a ton were unloaded there. The record added the happy sentence: 'Item: to them that helped to unload the boat and carry out the coals, and for ale at the unloading to the boatmen and others, 3s.'

Today, Grange is not a typical seaside resort, and it is all the better for that. The Promenade is beautifully kept, and the several gardens and small parks must be a comfort to the elderly people who spend some of their time looking out to the bay; and there is nothing of 'Morecambe' about this part of the bay! However, Grange is an active place, and I remember when I was appointed Writer-in-Residence for the Cumbria County Library, it was at Grange that my term of office began.

The small town is built on a hill, with houses tiered up the side of the fell in order that as many as possible may benefit from the magnificent view. It is said that during really exceptional conditions, it is possible to see Snowdon and the North Wales Coast, and the Isle of Man, from the hills around the town.

At the centre of Grange, by the Crown Hotel, the road swings northwards past the Clock Tower and St Paul's Church. The church was built over a period of two years, beginning in 1852, and it was consecrated on the 13th of October, 1853, by the Bishop of Chester. It is perhaps important to remember that until 1856 Cartmel and Furness, together with Kendal and its surrounding churches, were all part of the Chester Diocese. However, a year before the railway arrived at Grange, the parish became part of the Diocese of Carlisle.

It was an early vicar of Grange, Rev. H. R. Smith, who suggested that the place should be called Grange-over-Sands, so as to differentiate it from the other Grange, in Borrowdale. Possibly, the Vicar had in mind the experience of his predecessor, Rev. Mr Rigg, who had a narrow escape while crossing the sands. The details were included by Mary Wakefield in her *Cartmel Priory and Sketches of North Lonsdale*:

He returned to Manchester to make some final arrangements and sell a little property there, and succeeded in his object, but was all but lost in the Over-Sands coach when returning with his title deeds in his valise. The coach sank in a quick-sand and was rapidly settling down; the traces were cut, the horses taken out, and the passengers got safely off the sinking vehicle; when the coachman suddenly remembered there was one inside. The old gentleman was entirely oblivious to all that was going on, and being very delicate he had shut up all the windows, and muffled himself with so many rugs that he was only extricated with much difficulty through a window, the doors being fast in the sand. When placed on one of the horses new perils awaited him, for, not being much of a horseman, he slipped round degrees till at last he was quite underneath the animal, and finally found himself in the waters of the channel, the horse kicking him so severely on the shins that he was disabled for the whole winter.

The coach, after many months' disappearance in the sand, was finally washed up opposite Holme Island, having been gradually sucked along four or five miles distance. Mr Rigg's valise was recovered with the deeds and parchments therein scarcely legible, still sufficiently so to prove his rights of ownership.

It is surprising that Mr Rigg, much in the manner of Dr Foster's middling experiences at Gloucester, ever went to Grange again, but, of course, he could not get away except by taking the long roundabout route or crossing the sands again. Anything but that!

Lindale

Two possible roads lead from Grange to Lindale. The more westerly road passes by Eggerslack Wood, through which there are footpaths leading across to Hampsfield Fell. It is on Hampsfield or Hamps Fell that the strange-looking tower known as the Hospice is situated. This was built under the instructions of Rev. Thomas Remington, who became Vicar of Cartmel in 1830. The idea of the tower was to give shelter to any who wished to linger and take in the view, and was a generous gift from one who has been described as the 'most scholarly' of the Vicars of Cartmel, present company excepted! The top of Hamps Fell reminded me of Orton Scar with its exposed limestone and deep crevices with hart's tongue ferns growing deep down in the crevices; and it is a magnificent place from which to see the extent of Cartmel's southern coastline.

The alternative road, a relatively new road constructed in the nineteenth century, passes Blawith Point, and gives a good view of Holme Island, which is now linked to the mainland by a causeway. Before the Castle Head Marsh was drained and the River Winster made to flow down a canal-like channel, the island must have been cut off for much of the time, as must have Castle Head, at one time another island. This was once the home of John Wilkinson, the self-styled 'Father of Iron'. I can think of many things I would rather be father of, but then I have no ambition to match that of Wilkinson, who may well be the most important man to be associated with Cartmel, and Lindale, 'the lime valley', in particular.

John Wilkinson

John Wilkinson was the son of Isaac Wilkinson, who had settled at Backbarrow in about 1740, or a little earlier, to work in the iron-trade already established there. It is thought Isaac Wilkinson brought his two young sons, John and William, with him when he moved from Cumberland, and that he managed to develop his own small business, using molten iron from the larger furnace for his own moulds to make flat smoothing-irons. Possibly, it was the supervision of these private moulds that was John Wilkinson's first work; but evidently this side-line was successful, because by 1748, the Wilkinsons were able to purchase or build their own furnace at Wilson House, near Lindale. One of the first tasks undertaken was to dig a channel through the peat-moss, which would enable peat to be carried by water to the furnace, and it was the Wilkinsons' plan to use peat in the smelting process. The boat that floated on the channel was, according to tradition, made of iron, and as James Stockdale in his *Annales Caermoelenses* put it: 'This Wilson House Boat was really the parent of all the iron ships that have ever since been built – our noble-sided men-of-war, and that leviathan of ships, the *Great Eastern* herself, not excepted!'

In about 1755, John Wilkinson left Lindale and moved to Wolverhampton, though later he settled at Bilston, and it was while he was there that he met James Watt, whom he was able to help considerably by providing a bored cylinder for the famous steam-engine. In fact, Watt's first steam-engine had been ordered by Wilkinson to blow the bellows at the Iron Works at Broseley.

Soon the Wilkinsons owned several furnaces, and from their

works at Bersham guns were moulded and sent off to France, weapons which would eventually be aimed against the British troops during the Napoleonic Wars! However, in the Indian War, the British troops used Wilkinsons' howitzers, guns and shells.

In 1779, Wilkinson cast the first iron bridge which spanned the River Severn between Broseley and Madeley. It was one hundred feet and six inches in length, and weighed over three hundred and seventy tons.

The many achievements of John Wilkinson are beyond the scope of this book to relate, but perhaps I should mention his casting of the iron pipes for the Paris water supply and the building of iron barges that plied up and down the Severn. It would not be long before the Father of Iron's small railway, which he constructed to carry iron to the barges, would be imitated and developed into the great railway systems of the world.

The Father of Iron died on the 14th of July, 1808, at the age of 80, and he was interred in the grounds of Castle Head, after the hearse and four horses that were drawing his heavy coffin got entangled in the quicksands near Holme Island! The various toings and froings of Wilkinson's body until it reached its final resting place in Lindale churchyard make as bizarre reading as that of St Cuthbert! Today, the great twenty-ton pyramidal iron mausoleum may be seen in part standing near the corner of the Grange road, in Lindale. 'If gold rust, what shall iren do?', as the 'Father of English Poetry' asked on the way to Canterbury.

9

The Road to Lonsdale

I resolved to start the Westmorland Festival in 1885.
Mary Wakefield

The happy walker is able to cross over the Nether Bridge from Kirkland to Lound Road, something that many a driver might wish to do but is prevented from it by the Kendal one-way system. Anyone wishing to drive from the parish church, say, to Nether Street, a few yards away as the crow flies, is forced to go all the way round the town and cross the Kent by Miller Bridge, often meeting hooting frustrations on the way! The walker, meanwhile, has nipped across Nether Bridge and is out of sight.

The Nether, or 'Lower', Bridge was first recorded in the thirteenth century when it was referred to as 'Caput Pontis', in 1210; this would have been a wooden structure placed beside the ford for pedestrians to use. However, it was almost certainly a stone bridge for which, in 1376, a grant of pontage was made for repairs covering a three-year period, and in the document the bridge is described as being broken down. At that time it would have been exceedingly narrow, wide enough only for pedestrians and horses to cross, and carts and waggons would have continued to use the ford close by. By 1582, the bridge was in busy use and an order was given that 'no person or persons from henceforth shall or may, either draw or trail any timber or other draught whatsoever either by strength of horses or other cattle or by power of men above one beast draught, at any one time'.

It was not until almost two hundred years later, in 1772, that the bridge was considerably widened. The work was completed by the summer, but in the autumn there was a disaster, for the Kent rose so high after several days of incessant rain that, on the 29th of October, the new work was washed away! However, it seems the damage was speedily repaired, although for a while, no doubt, people were splashing across the ford.

Nether Bridge was a tollbridge, and the office of Bridgetoller was very profitable. The rent paid in 1812 was £377, but with increasing traffic as people began to visit the Lakes the toll rent had risen in eight years to £700!

Until 1906, there was a small row of cottages, the malt-kiln cottages, situated on the west side of the bridge. These appear in several early photographs of the town, as does the Netherfield Toll House which stood at the junction between the Burton and Natland roads.

The mention of Netherfield makes any Kendalian think immediately of shoes, but even those who know little or nothing about Kendal will know of K Shoes, and although the Japanese may think of Karate Shoes, the Americans of Kansas Shoes, and the Arabs of Kurdistan Shoes, we know the secret and think of Kendal!

K Shoes is proud of starting in one small room. This was in 1842, when Robert Somervell began his small leather business. In this he was following a trade which had long been established in the town, and, indeed, the Kendal shoemakers, as I have already mentioned, gave their name to Soutergate. In 1661, the shoemakers of Carlisle bought from Kendal 331 pairs of shoes, which cost them £35 16s. 7d. No doubt, this was to meet some special demand, but they seem to have known K Shoes were the ones to buy.

In 1844, Somervell moved to larger premises, so successful had he been in the two preceding years; the larger house was near the east end of Nether Bridge. What was Somervell up to? 'Up' was the operative word for what he was making were the uppers and leathers for other shoemakers, and, in 1847, Robert Somervell was joined by his brother, John, and several other workers, for all the cutting and stitching was at that time done by hand. However, ten years later sewing machines imported from America would revolutionize the shoe trade. It is said the Kendal folk were sceptical about the new invention, and the Somervell brothers called a special meeting, which was, in fact, more like a party, in the Town Hall. During the meeting one of the workers introduced 'a special guest', what he described as their best friend, and dramatically lifted the cover from one of the new machines! Their salvation was here, he announced; this would mean more money for all. It was hardly salvation, but it was the beginning of K Shoes' success, so that in 1862 the Somervell venture won a Bronze Medal at the London Industrial Exhibition, an honour celebrated by a grand open-air ball and a trip up the canal from Kendal to Levens!

Robert Somervell was to see his works at Netherfield expand, and in 1862 also, the first completed shoes were made, so that when he died in 1899 he must have known he had started something that would go from strength to strength.

In 1950, K Shoes became a public company, and eleven years later, with several new factories opened in the North, the company acquired W. H. H. Clark's, of Norwich. However, the name of 'Clark' would soon loom large in the company's destiny, for K Shoes would eventually be taken over themselves by C & J Clark Ltd. Today it is a subsidiary of that larger concern. It seems a good bet to start on one's uppers!

Oxenholme

Oxenholme, 'the water-meadow where oxen were pastured', has always been closely linked with Kendal and, indeed, considered part of it from earliest times. Situated barely two miles from the castle under the shelter of a high, long narrow ridge, the Helm, Oxenholme was good grazing land, and it is mentioned, in 1274, as one of the farms owned by Robert de Roos, of Kendal Castle. However, nobody could have guessed how familiar the name 'Oxenholme' was destined to become once the Lancaster to Carlisle Railway was built in the 1840s, though it was a touch-and-go matter, for the station was originally called Kendal Junction. Even today the kind of people who will not leave things alone are talking of renaming the station 'Kendal South'. They might at least in the cause of accuracy talk of 'Kendal South-East'. I for one will be a staunch supporter of the 'Keep Oxenholme' campaign, which, if it does not yet exist, I hope soon will!

Today, as in the case of K Shoes, there are thousands of people who know Oxenholme yet know very little or nothing about Kendal: all those who know it as just one more stop on the way to London or Glasgow; another platform to watch the waving greetings, farewells, whistles and slamming doors. However, some will remember that Oxenholme came into the news when, some twenty years ago, a policeman was shot dead at the station.

The decision to take the main line through Oxenholme, and so avoid the town of Kendal, was simply a matter of engineering. The line begins to climb somewhere east of Milnthorpe and continues in a steady gradient towards Grayrigg, Tebay and Shap. To have taken the line through Kendal, once the alternative plan to take it up Longsleddale had been shelved, would have meant losing the advantage.

The existence of the railway meant that Oxenholme itself would develop and, I would imagine, there may be many people, particularly those who approach the station from the north and east, who have never seen the houses and little shops of Oxenholme! One could not really apply the term 'village' to the place, but there is more there than one might expect.

The road from Kendal to Burton, the A65, takes a southerly route and bypasses several villages, so that Natland, Sedgwick and Stainton are relatively little known if compared with Staveley, say, or Grayrigg. However, there is an alternative route which takes in these villages and is very much more relaxing on the nerves than roaring up and down the A65 or, even worse, the A 591 (T), which is the fastest way to travel from Crooklands to Kendal; what one might even call the 'crooks' road! Anyway, it is the small road from Kendal to Natland that passes the site of the Roman fort at Watercrook, so perhaps this is the 'crooks' road after all. Speaking of roads, it seems a good moment to say something more about the Romans whose occupation of Westmorland, one must remember, was of a military nature only.

The Romans needed an efficient system of well-constructed roads which would enable troops to move quickly and without interference. So a line of forts and smaller stations were established along each major route. There were two major roads from the South which converged at Brougham, a little to the south of Penrith. The westerly road came up the Lune Valley and, where it concerns us, had a station at Overborough, south-east of Kirkby Lonsdale, and another at Low Borrow Bridge, near Tebay. It then continued over Shap Fell through Crosby Ravensworth and on to Brougham. The other road, the north-eastern route from York to Carlisle, went up the Eden Valley with major stations at Brough and Kirkby Thore. Besides these there were many lesser roads, though not less remarkable, such as the one I mentioned earlier from Brougham to Ambleside, which crossed over High Street. The road which passed through Watercrook, the station the Roman's called 'Alauna', was probably a minor link-road from Lancaster, via Burrow, in Lonsdale, and Watercrook, to Low Borrow Bridge. There was possibly another road in Furness linked with Lancaster by the over-sands route, for it may be the sands crossing that Agricola described in a letter to his famous son-in-law, Tacitus, as a dangerous passage his troops had taken in AD 79.

The station of Alauna at Watercrook extended over some four acres and was built of stone, which means it was a permanent position. Excavation work carried out at various times revealed several items pointing to an occupation lasting from the time of the Emperor Domitian, who ruled from AD 81 to 96, until about 340, when the fort seems to have been abandoned. Many of the Roman 'finds' may be seen in the Kendal Museum.

It is just possible that the fort was destroyed by a fire, which caused the place to be abandoned, for when Thomas Machell visited the site in 1692 he found the foundations of houses in abundance, 'which we may conclude were destroyed by fire by the black, sooty colour of the mould cast up within these precincts of the fort, which is contrary to the soil of that country'. Machell records many interesting details of what the Romans would have needed most in the winter months: a hypocaust, a Roman central heating system!

Natland
As Natland is situated so near to Oxenholme there may be good reasons for thinking that Natland is a form of 'neat's land', another grazing place for neats or cattle, but none of the early spellings of the name point to this. In fact, even the 'land' part is not what one might expect since it comes from the Old Norse *lund* meaning a small wood, though often indicating a sacred grove of some sort. The 'Nat' part could either be a personal name of Norse origin, 'Nati's Wood', or it could be 'nettle wood', or even 'the wet wood'!

It will be noticed by some that I have excluded the possibility that the name of Natland has anything to do with Kendal Castle and those who lived outside its confines, but the *nativi* must go the way of the neats!

Natland is today an attractive little place, if one stands on the village green and looks about. There are fine old houses and an impressive-looking church, which is, in fact, fairly young, and another of Paley and Austin's designs, built in 1909. The fact that Natland was a chapelry of Kendal would have meant that, like many of the other places I have mentioned, there would have been a chapel of some kind there in mediaeval times. It is known that in 1680 the chapel was in a state of dilapidation, and it was pulled down in 1735, when another was built on the site with a graveyard added. However, a much larger church was built in 1825, and this in turn was enlarged in 1879.

The present church, St Mark's, has a particularly interesting and instructive east window. This is modern and was placed in memory of Sub.-Lieut Ernest Maples RNVR who was killed in 1944, aged nineteen. The theme of the window is the Benedictus with Christ reigning from the tree of life, but what I liked about it was the many contemporary figures included: nurses, bus-drivers, munitions workers, firemen and railwaymen, besides the more expected soldiers and sailors.

Once one turns away from the village green one might be in any suburbs with rather smart-looking modern houses. Here are Abbey Drive, Robby-Lea-Drive, but I did not dare look any further!

Sedgwick

Also situated on the east bank of the Kent is Sedgwick, a small township through which the old Lancaster to Kendal Canal used to pass. The last stretch of the canal, opened in 1819, linked Kendal with the southern section, which had opened in 1796, and it was of convenience to the gunpowder-mill which the Wakefield family ran in Sedgwick for over a hundred years, and later when the business was transferred to Gatebeck.

Although Sedgwick was considered as part of Heversham for civil purposes, ecclesiastically it was in Crosscrake Parish, but it was largely, if not entirely, owing to the Wakefields that Sedgwick developed as a village, for they not only ran the gunpowder-mill but also commissioned our old friends Paley and Austin to design a stately home. This large Gothic-style mansion, Sedgwick House, was completed in 1869, and the good architects also designed the furnishings! It was here that the most famous Wakefield, Mary Wakefield, spent much of her childhood, and her musical career and the festival that she founded deserve close attention.

The Wakefields were Quakers. If not all members were of the strictest kind, it has been said that the Quaker movement was the 'bed-rock on which their convictions were founded, and an active principle in their daily lives'. Mary Wakefield's great-grandfather, John Wakefield, founded the bank in Kendal which bore the family name, though it was often referred to as the Kendal Bank. The bank continued in the family until it was bought by the Bank of Liverpool in 1893. Mary's father, William Henry Wakefield, entered the bank as a young man and in 1851 married Augusta Hagarty, the daughter of the American Consul to Liverpool, and settled in one of the family houses, the Old Bank House in Stricklandgate, where Mary was born on the 19th of August, 1853. Mary always claimed that it was from her American mother than she inherited her musical gift.

In 1858, William Wakefield built a country house for his family near Sedgwick, at Prizett, but in 1866 he inherited Sedgwick House, and it was he who instigated the Paley and Austin designs for a complete rebuilding. Mary was sixteen when the family moved to Sedgwick and very soon afterwards she was sent to a finishing school in Brighton where she received music lessons from two gentlemen with splendid sounding names: Mr Kuhe and Signor Meccatti. 'Here, in fact,' wrote Mary in later life, 'I first heard any music at all, to speak of, and it was indeed the opening up of heaven.'

Mary's first public performance as a singer was given in 1873 when she sang in a concert on behalf of a hospital scheme organized by her aunt, Mrs Cropper of Ellergreen: among the songs she sang were Sullivan's 'Once Again' and 'Sad Heart, Now Take Thy Rest' by Virginia Gabriel.

By 1876 Mary Wakefield was in London having her voice trained by Professor Randegger, learning harmony from a Professor Bannister, the piano from Sir William Cusins, and also the violin. It was during this period in London, lodging with

Market day – Kirkby Lonsdale
Memories of Hutton Roof

friends, that the main part of her musical education was accomplished. She joined the Amateur Musical Guild and the Handel Society, but was refused admission by the Bach Society. These former gave her her early solo experience. 'I never sang [solo] in public', she wrote, 'except in some very tiny affairs till I was twenty, and I first sang in London at a semi-public concert at Lambeth Palace, in 1876, in the day of Archbishop Tait.'

The spring and autumn were spent in London; the rest of the year at Sedgwick where she entertained, with her parents' approval, many musical friends. Soon she was in demand for concerts all over the country and besides London, she sang in Blackpool, Gloucester and Torquay. In 1878, the year she went out to Rome with her parents, she made a tour with engagements in Mansfield, Retford, Worksop, Nottingham and Chester. In Rome Mary studied under Signor Alari, a famous teacher of the time, and gave a charity concert in the Sala Dante where she received her first bouquet. 'Her voice is marvellous in its wonderfully even quality. The notes linger on the air like the tones of a finely-vibrating stringed instrument, and I do not think I ever heard a purer, more perfectly graduated register. Her style is so large and fine, so utterly without coquetry or trick of voice,' wrote Baroness von Rabe another pupil.

In the September of 1879 Mary was the contralto soloist at the Gloucester Festival in Leonardo Leo's *Dixit Dominus*. This success, for all the reviews were favourable, might have prompted her to take singing professionally, except that the conventions of the time would have made it very difficult. It was considered unjustifiable for a woman of means to earn money when in doing so she might be depriving someone else of a living. So it was that at her parents' wish she declined opportunities to sing at the Chester, Norwich and Leeds Festivals.

In the autumn of 1884, a concert was given in the small village school at Preston Patrick at which the plans to hold a singing competition the following year were announced. This would be at Sedgwick, where the first Mary Wakefield Festival took place on the tennis court in the grounds of Sedgwick House. The test piece selected was Stevens's 'Ye Spotted Snakes'; three quartets took part. Dr Brown was the Judge and Mary

Winter floodwater near Burton

Wakefield gave away the prize. The following year there were more events, twenty-one entries in all, and so the competition was transferred from Sedgwick to St George's Hall, Kendal. Known as the Sedgwick Choral Competition, it later became in 1891, after the death of Mary's father, the Wakefield Choral Competition. Claims have been made for this festival being the first of its kind, but such claims are inaccurate. It is true that this kind of choral competition spread quickly to other towns, but Mary herself admitted that the idea had come from her friend Henry Leslie who had begun the Herefordshire Philharmonic Society some twenty-five years earlier: 'We both felt,' Mary wrote, 'that the stimulus of competition was a valuable vital initiative, and we thought that the many evils that follow in its wake might be to a great extent avoided. So we passed on to plans and ways and means, and I resolved to start the Westmorland Festival in 1885.'

The competition was an annual event until 1906 when it became a biennial one, which it has remained to this day. The effect of the festival was to stimulate interest in music generally, and winter concerts were often held in Kendal. Performers like Clara Butt, Myra Hess and Adila Fachiri have been heard in the town over the years, besides the Hallé and the BBC Northern Orchestras.

Each year of the festival a guest conductor is invited to conduct the Festival Choir in a celebratory concert, and these have included Sir Henry Wood, Sir Malcolm Sargent and Sir Adrian Boult, and just about every famous name you could think of in the list of conductors. In 1981, Sir Donald Hunt conducted the choir in Leonard Bernstein's *Chichester Psalms* and Bach's Chorale from *Sleepers Wake*, and the Festival Orchestra, which was drawn from members of the BBC Scottish Orchestra, played Schubert's Fifth Symphony. In the competition there were 57 different classes of entry. Not bad for such small beginnings!

Mary Wakefield died in the autumn of 1910. Perhaps, what she felt about it all is best summed up by her comments on the Festival of 1906: 'I felt that the taste of performers and audience had been steadily raised when two movements of Beethoven's C Minor Symphony were encored vociferously by a chorus of 500 villagers from the dales and fells of Westmorland.'

Crosscrake

I mentioned that Sedgwick was in Crosscrake, the name being an inverted form of 'Kraki's cross', but we shall never know much about Kraki beyond the fact that he was another of the Norsemen to lend his name to the area. Perhaps a community formed itself round this centre of Christian worship, for Sedgwick is 'Sigge's dairy-farm' and Stainton, the 'Stone farmstead'.

The first chapel at Crosscrake was founded in the reign of Richard I by Anselm de Furness, though it was later granted to the Canons of Cartmel Priory by Sir William Strickland during the reign of Edward I. When Machell passed by in 1692 the chapel was in use as a school, which was a common practice when there was no special school building; but he made several other alarming observations in his usual note form:

> The Chapel – nine long – five broad – but it has been much longer – salary – none: nor prayers read – no dedication. There was once a bell but now none, nor place for a bell. The bell sold to make a school-house. Was repaired eight years since, by a contribution – ruined in the Civil War – they gave £12 per annum. No quire – no seats.

I must confess to finding Machell's notes extremely funny, and I do not understand exactly the situation concerning the school-house. Perhaps the bell was sold in order to carry out sufficient repairs to make the chapel suitable for the children to be taught inside, for, if there was a separate schoolhouse, why were the children being taught in the chapel? Whatever the facts, Machell went on to record theat the Crosscrake children were 'well-faced'; but after such distressing information about the chapel one is hardly surprised that his next port of call was the Maidenhead Inn!

It is in Crosscrake Parish that a small beck rises which eventually becomes the River Bela. In its early stages the stream is called St Sunday's Beck, a strange name with an interesting, not to say amusing, origin; for St Sunday is, in fact, St Dominic, and the confusion arose from the Latin 'Dominicus' being so alike the Latin for Sunday: *dominica*! I have a feeling our forefathers would have laughed at the joke, and there is a St Sunday's Crag in Patterdale.

St Sunday's Beck rises on the fells north-east of New Hutton, a small hamlet some three miles east of Oxenholme and a little to the south of Lambrigg and Docker, which I spoke about in a previous chapter. Hutton, 'the farmstead on the hill', is situated in the 'hay', that is, the hunting lands east of Kendal Castle. Anyone who visits New Hutton will notice one distinctive feature, the figures of greyhounds on the pillars of the church gate, and a gateway that leads into the old school. The greyhounds are more memorable than the little church designed by George Webster in 1828 and dedicated to St Stephen.

At one time there was a large house, Sleddall Hall, situated on the north side of the hamlet, but nothing of this remains and only a slightly higher wall is noticeable on the side of the road. This was once the wall of the kitchen-garden. Nevertheless, there are several attractive houses to be seen in a place which might well be overlooked, and it is good to know there are still greyhounds coursing in the hay, even if they are destined never to collide!

Hincaster

Hincaster, a township in Heversham Parish, is situated between Stainton and Heversham, being some two miles northeast of the latter. Although they will not know it by name, Hincaster must be a familiar sight to those who travel by train and see it from the carriage window as the track begins to climb slowly by Milnthorpe towards Oxenholme. For those who live in this somewhat secluded little village one of the problems must be the noise of these trains!

Hincaster is listed in Domesday Book, where it appears as 'Hennecastre', and the name seems to denote some Roman presence, the name meaning the 'fortification haunted by hens'. No Roman remains of any kind have been found, but it is thought that there might have been a road from Carnforth to Watercrook which passed through Hincaster and Stainton, and that there was some kind of Roman settlement or camp at Hincaster. Whatever the circumstances, there is no doubt but that the name is derived from the Latin *castra* and that, although Hincaster is today a place to pass by, either by rail or by the fast A59(T) between Crooklands and Kendal, the Romans may have lingered there and scattered corn for their hens!

The mention of Crooklands brings us to Preston Richard, once an extensive township of Heversham which contained the hamlets of Birkrigg Park, Endmoor, Milton, Low Park and the village of Crooklands itself. It was at Crooklands that the Wigan coal owner, the Earl of Crawford and Belcarres, had a large wharf on the Kendal Canal and a range of coke ovens, during the latter part of the last century.

Preston Richard takes its name from a Richard de Preston, one of the early lords of the manor, the same family that owned Holker Hall.

Preston Patrick

Preston Patrick is a large township which consists of four small hamlets, Gatebeck, Goose Green, Millness and Nook, and it was in the parish of Burton-in-Kendal until it became a parish in its own right.

Preston, 'the priest's farmstead', was the place where Thomas, son of Gospatrick, founded an abbey for the Premonstratensian Order. It has been suggested the Patrick from whom the place takes its name was a member of the same family, possibly a grandson of Thomas, Patrick de Curwen, an ancestor of the Curwens of Workington.

It seems the position of the abbey was unsatisfactory, and the community moved to Shap, where it remained until the Dissolution, in 1539. There are no signs at Preston Patrick of the old abbey; but as the abbey was here it might be of interest if I said something about its foundation. It is fairly certain that there was some kind of religious community in existence already, and Preston is mentioned in Domesday Book as one of the manors of Torfin, so the association with the priest had begun before the end of the eleventh century. Now, the date given for the abbey's foundation by Thomas is usually 1119, and this date was adopted by Dr Burn, the author of the Westmorland part of *The History and Antiquities of Westmorland and Cumberland*, but it could not possibly be as early as that. The Premonstratensians were not founded until 1121! The Premonstratensians were canons regular according to the so-called rule of St Augustine, which I mentioned in connection with Cartmel, and took their name from Prémontré, the abbey, near Laon in France, built by St Norbert on a spot revealed to him by the Virgin Mary in a vision: hence the name, 'shown before'. This, as I say, was in

1121, and the Canons of Prémontré became known as Norbertines, or White Canons. The order grew rapidly, and after only some thirty years there were about a hundred abbeys, some of which were in England and Scotland. The first English house was situated at Newhouse, in Lincolnshire, in 1143. Newhouse founded another abbey at Croxton, in Leicestershire, from which was founded Cockersand Abbey, situated on the mouth of the River Lune, in 1190. Croxton also founded Blanchland in Northumberland, in 1165, and it was from that house that the canons came to Preston Patrick, but when? One thing is certain it was not 1119, and it must have been after 1165.

When it was decided that the site at Shap on the east bank of the River Lowther was more secluded, and better in every way, the canons moved and settled there in 1208. They were beholden to the senior house at Cockersand as it was considered easier to administer the abbey from there than from Blanchland, over the Pennines.

My suggestion would be that Preston Patrick was always intended as a temporary base from which a suitable site could be reconnoitred, and that an old religious house, probably at the time abandoned, was conveniently to hand.

Travellers on the northbound carriageway of the M6 may have noticed St Gregory's Church, perched on its little hill, as they pass Junction 36. One of the yew trees in the churchyard is considerably older than the church itself which was built in 1852, with a chancel being added some forty years later. Standing in that little churchyard and watching the traffic grinding up and down the motorway gave me a sense of sanity and permanence, and a feeling of irony that here, amidst the roar and the moan I was looking down towards Preston Patrick Hall, now a farmhouse, and only a stone's throw from the famous Quaker Meeting House which is so associated with quietism; but to be a quietist one does not need quiet, for the spirit of God came like a mighty rushing wind!

10

Kirkby Lonsdale

Long stand the bridge – long flow the Lune
The Toast of Kirkby Lonsdale

The Lonsdale Ward of the Kendal Barony, situated at the south-east of the county and bordering with the West Riding of Yorkshire and Lancashire, was very much the smallest of the four wards. It contained, nevertheless, two market towns: Kirkby Lonsdale and Burton, of which the former was always the more important, and included in its parish the townships of Hutton Roof, Lupton, Mansergh, Killington, Firbank, Dillicar, Middleton, Barbon and Casterton; while Burton, known as Burton-in-Kendal, included two townships only, Holme and Dalton.

Kirkby Lonsdale appears in Domesday Book as 'Cherchebi' and, together with Middleton, Lupton, Mansergh and Hutton Roof, is listed as among the twelve manors held by Thane Torfin. However, it was not long afterwards that Ivo de Tailbois gained possession and gave the church, lands and common rights away to St Mary's Abbey, York, in the same way that he had given Kendal, as we have seen.

This donation to York was restricted to the ecclesiastical lands and rights only; the manor de Tailbois continued to hold himself, although he seems to have let it out to a family that called itself de Kirkby, after the place. Between the years 1231 and 1240, the exact date is undetermined, John de Kirkby entered the priesthood and handed over his manorial rights to St Mary's Abbey, but not before he had been granted a charter by the Crown to hold a weekly market on a Thursday, and an annual fair on the eve, day and morrow of the Feast of the Nativity of Our Lady, that is, the 7th, 8th and 9th of September.

The market charter is significant not only because it is early compared with many places but because it set Kirkby Lonsdale on the way to becoming an important market town, though visitors to the town, today, must not be misled by the Market Square, which is not really all that old, having been formed only in 1832! The ancient market was held in Market Street, in the vicinity of the church; this is approached from the present Market Square a few hundred yards up Main Street, and is the most attractive part of the town. Market Street leads into Queen's Square, a Victorian development, and on into Fair-bank, a street where the fairs are thought to have extended and where the horses and carts used to be 'parked' on market days.

The old market cross, which stands at present in a small square, once the swine market, used at one time to be situated in the middle of the street where Main Street and Market Street meet. It is one of the delightful features of the town, and remains to remind one of the town's past. I say this, because of all the towns in Westmorland Kirkby Lonsdale is 'refined', even a guide book informs us that the annual fair, something which had lasted in the town for close on eight hundred years, was 'discontinued because of the undesirable elements it attracted to the town'. It is the 'undesirable elements' that are today lacking! Almost every shop has a door or window crusted with credit cards, those odious advertisements that fortunately Appleby has so far resisted, though one hears frequent talk of 'undesirable elements' at the time of the Appleby Horse Fair:

I suppose Kirkby Lonsdale is famous for two things: Ruskin's View and the Devil's Bridge. As to Ruskin's View I have never really seen what all the fuss is about, but then living where I do I suppose I have become blasé. There are many places where the Lune looks just as impressive, particularly the stretch from Tebay to its meeting with the River Rawthay, a mile or so south of Sedbergh. No, Ruskin went into raptures because Turner had painted the view from the churchyard in 1822, and, for Ruskin, Turner was 'sent as a prophet of God to reveal to men the mysteries of His universe'. For Ruskin all God's skies were Turner's skies, and not the other way round! The famous view is approached best from the churchyard, if one is in a hurry; a narrow made-up path, Fisherty Brow, leads towards the gazebo which Turner managed to include in his painting. However, the way I would choose would be to take the footpath from the Devil's Bridge and walk along the river bank to the steps which will take one up to the gazebo. This way one has the benefit of being able to look back at the view. On the other hand, one could always leave the view out altogether and go straight to the Devil's Bridge, which really is worth seeing.

This bridge was built some time during the reign of Edward III, about 1370 or so, by the monks of St Mary's Abbey, York, in order to replace the earlier wooden bridge which had fallen into a state of disrepair. This earlier bridge was the subject of a grant of pontage for six years given to the Vicar of Kirkby Lonsdale, Richard de Wisebeche, in 1365, and it is thought to have been situated at the old ford across what is known as Far Lune.

The name by which the bridge is known, the Devil's Bridge, has been ascribed to a legend of the nineteenth century, but surely it is older than that! It was common for monasteries to build and maintain bridges, just as they maintained the roads if they passed through monastery land. This was done in one of two ways: either a bridge was built with alms, special sums donated for the purpose, which was the most usual way, and most small bridges were of this sort, or the Abbot could choose to build a bridge out of monastery funds and not call upon donations. In France such bridges built without alms were known as *ponts maudit* or *ponts diable*, and in England, it seems, *devil's bridges*.

As a result of the bridge's name, various legends sprang up in the nineteenth century, or slightly earlier, in which bizarre tales of women with baskets of cakes or buns and little dogs, cows and ponies appear. However, the Devil has never built anything that did not soon collapse and the Bridge at Kirkby Lonsdale is as sturdy as a rock, and on a rock did the Lord of All build His church! It was said in 1870 that 'the country people have a tradition that the bridge was built by the Devil in windy weather. He had but one apronful of stones for the purpose, and unfortunately, his apron strings breaking as he flew over Casterton Fell, he lost many of them out, or the bridge would have been wider.' 'Windy weather'? No, all hot air.

Queen Elizabeth School
This famous school founded towards the end of Queen Elizabeth's reign in 1591 was originally situated on Mill Brow, the

former King's Street and the old coach road. Edward Godsalve of
the Parish of Whittington had donated £100 for the endowment
of a school, and together with other endowments, including one
from Lady Elizabeth Curwen of Old Biggins Hall, who gave the
site, the first building was erected, though it was found necessary to rebuild the school as early as 1628. This rebuilding work
was paid for by Henry Wilson of Underley who further endowed the school in many ways providing scholarships for four
boys to go up to Queen's College, Oxford; while his brother, Rev.
Thomas Wilson, provided three scholarships to Christ's College,
Cambridge. These were in each case for the sons of those who
otherwise could not afford the expense.

For two hundred years or so the school remained on Mill
Brow, until, in 1846, the school was moved to Springfield a new
site north of the town where a new school and master's house
were built. Here the place continued to grow steadily and is still
flourishing today with many new buildings. The earlier school-
room is now the school library and the Headmaster's House
provides a suitable boarding-house, for those few who live too
far away to come to the school daily.

Underley Hall

It is near the small hamlet of Kearstwick, 'the valley clearing',
that Underley Hall, one of the most illustrious houses in the
district, is situated, standing in extensive parkland. Described
at the time of its building in 1825 as 'a mansion more splendid
than any in the county with the exception of Lowther Castle'.
The exception of Lowther was tactful in the extreme, since Lord
Lonsdale was Lord of the Manor! The instigator of this mock
Jacobean pile was Alexander Nowell, an Indian Army officer,
who had bought the estate in 1825, when fairly small in size.
Nowell commissioned the Kendal architect, George Webster, to
design a mansion fitting his aspirations, and Webster set to
work on a plan which involved demolishing the house that
already stood on the site and replacing it with Underley.

Nowell seems to have been a property developer, and over the
succeeding years bought all the farms he could that bordered on
the estate, so that when he came to sell it in 1840 to William
Thompson, a city merchant from London, the acreage was vast.
In 1864, Thompson's grandson, the Earl of Bective, inherited

Underley and remained there until he died, in 1893. The estate then comprised some 25,000 acres, and was passed to his daughter, Lady Henry Cavendish-Bentinck, whose husband was the half-brother of the Duke of Portland. There are many people in the Kirkby Lonsdale area who well remember Lord and Lady Cavendish-Bentinck being at the hall, and one or two I talked to had been born and brought up on the estate. Lord Henry, who had served as Member of Parliament for South Nottinghamshire for many years, died in 1931, and his wife in 1939.

Underley Hall is an ideal building to house a school, and that has been its role ever since the Cavendish-Bentinck's time, though the estate still belongs to the family. The hall saw service first as Hordle House, a boy's preparatory school, then as Oakfield, a girl's boarding school. In 1959, it became St Michael's College, a seminary for the Roman Catholic Diocese of Lancaster, and when this closed down the hall became what it still is, a school for boys, particularly for those 'who find life difficult'.

Knowing that the family still owned the land, I was not too surprised to come across several thousand pheasants in pens being fed by two proud-looking gamekeepers when I took the wrong path to the hall over an extravagant bridge that spanned the Lune. The pheasants looked content, as though they, at least, found life easy, but then it was after the 1st of February!

Mansergh

The most direct road from Kirkby Lonsdale to Kendal, though not the fastest is the B6254. It passes through three places: Old Town, Old Hutton, and Oxenholme. Old Town is the chief hamlet in the township of Mansergh, a wide area mentioned in Domesday Book as among the estates of Torfin. The meaning of the name is obscure; at least, the first element is. The 'ergh' part comes from the Old Norse for a dairy-farm as we have seen already, in Sizergh and Skelsmergh. It has been suggested the 'Man' may be derived from a personal name of some kind, but nothing is known more than that.

Old Town is an odd collection of houses, and particularly noticeable is the large house called Terry Bank. This was built by the Conder family, who settled there during the reign of Henry VII. A Richard Conder, of Old Town, Mansergh, was

buried in Kirkby Lonsdale churchyard, in 1542, a date displayed on the outside of the present house. As the other date
displayed is 1910, I can only suppose that the house is what it,
indeed, looks, a twentieth-century 'mock-up', but, as I say, it is
noticeable!

A road eastwards from the village leads to St Peter's Church,
built by Paley and Austin, in 1880, in the late Perpendicular
style. The church stands on a small eminence, with attractive
countryside around, and I found Mansergh, like Preston Patrick, a good place to linger. The most distinctive feature of the
church is the west tower with its saddleback roof, but the
churchyard is well stocked with yews, and a gate into the field
leads along an old road which links the church with Mansergh
Hall, from where there is a fine view of the River Lune. However, the made-up road by the old school building, is the one
most people will take, not ignoring the exhortation *Laus Deo*
displayed on the school with the date 1839, one hopes. This road
joins another that runs parallel with the river, though it fails to
imitate the sudden cavort the Lune manages by Holme House.
Here is a crook, if ever there was one! Soon the road passes the
ruins of Rigmaden Park, once a large mansion built by Christopher Wilson, of Abbot Hall, in Kendal. This work was begun in
1829, and Rigmaden was built on the site of an earlier house
which Wilson had purchased four years previously, together
with the manorial rights. Rigmaden, 'the maiden's ridge', com-
mands a magnificent view of the Middleton and Barbon Fells,
and rather aptly gazes back towards Casterton where the
famous girls' school is still very much alive.

Casterton School was founded by Rev. William Carus-Wilson
at Cowan Bridge, in 1823. This was situated on the road between Kirkby Lonsdale and Ingleton, and there being no church
there the girls used to walk across the fell to Tunstall, a distance
of nearly four miles. The school was intended for the daughters
of the clergy, and until 1921, when the restriction was lifted, it
was known as the Clergy Daughters' School. The school had
moved away from Cowan Bridge in 1833 to a more favourable
site in Casterton, and more convenient, since the Carus-Wilsons
owned Casterton Hall.

Casterton's most celebrated pupil, so far, is Charlotte Brontë,
who, together with her sisters, Maria, Elizabeth and Emily,

attended the school while it was at Cowan Bridge. In fact, in 1824, all four girls were at the school at one time! The grim establishment Charlotte Brontë describes as Lowood in *Jane Eyre* was based on the school and bears no resemblance, one hastens to add, to the school of today, where all remember, in the words of their famous sister, that 'Conventionality is not morality, Self-righteousness is not religion.'

The road from Rigmaden, where the park was described, in 1905, as being well-stocked with red and fallow deer, leads to the next Kirkby Lonsdale township, Killington.

Killington

Killington is a familiar name to those travelling on the southbound carriageway of the M6, for there is a service station there is a fine position looking out on to the Killington Reservoir, a large artificial lake created to supply water for the Kendal and Lancaster Canal, in 1820.

The reservoir, which belongs to the British Waterways Board, is some three miles or so from the small hamlet of Killington but is separated from it by a fairly large area of forest land, in a region known as the Old Park. Killington is well worth seeing and it probably seldom is. It is in a deep valley where a small beck, Springs Gill, suddenly turns southwards for a while, before continuing its easterly course towards the Lune. Here, Killington Hall is set down a narrow lane, with All Saint's Church opposite. The hall was the home of the Pickering family for many generations, and the first member of the family to be recorded as holding the manor was William Pickering, who was granted Killington by Peter de Brus, during the reign of Henry III, in return for an annual gift of a pair of gilt spurs, or their equivalent. Pickering was also to pay 6d at the Feast of Pentecost, and 'the military service of the 20th part of a knight's fee when occasion should require'. Several members of this family represented the shire in Parliament, and it was they who built the hall as a fortified dwelling. Later, in 1640, the Kitson family built a manor house which incorporated some of the earlier building, although it was the Uptons who, in 1803, made many alterations, as the initials IU indicate.

The church opposite the hall was built as a chapel served from Kirkby Lonsdale, in the fourteenth century. Although it has been rebuilt several times, it gives the impression of age. The west tower was built in 1711. What I liked most about this delightful little church, however, were the old oil lamps, a feature so often removed from such places, but I did notice there were several spotlights placed discreetly, high on the rafters!

Killington is nearer to Sedbergh than it is to Kirkby Lonsdale, and, indeed, several of the Kirkby Lonsdale townships are considerable distances from the main town, but none is further than Dillicar.

Dillicar

Dillicar is the most northerly township of the Lonsdale Ward, but to all intents and purposes it was considered as part of Grayrigg in the Kendal Parish; and when the London and North-Western Railway was routed through from Oxenholme to Tebay the place seemed even more naturally to belong to Kendal, something which the placing of the M6 was to endorse. However, it was the course of the River Lune that determined the matter at the beginning, for, although the railway and the motorway follow the river through what is called the Lune Valley Gorge, at Lowgill they soon swing away westwards from the river which continues more or less due south.

The place seems to mean the 'acre of land growing with dill or vetches' and the earliest record spells the name 'Dylacre'. The area is dominated by Dillicar Knott which rises some 1,144 feet above sea-level, but is insignificant; if compared with the Howgills on the opposite side of the river.

Dillicar contains one small hamlet, Beckfoot. Here the Ingleton Line crossed over Lowgill Viaduct which spans Deep Gill, a small tributary of the Lune that joins the larger river near the Crook O'Lune Bridge. This bridge is very old and links Dillicar and Firbank with Howgill, on the east side of the river. At one time the waters of Deep Gill turned the mill at Davy Bank, but the mill-house is still occupied and is in a most attractive position. In 1274, 'a moiety of the mill at Dylaker is worth 10s. yearly' appears in a list of the estates of Robert de Roos, of Kendal Castle.

Lowgill Station, which was the junction between the Ingleton Line and the London and North-Western Railway, and the

many railway cottages that were built beside it, meant that
Lowgill became a more familiar name than either Beckfoot or
Dillicar, and at the beginning of this century there were seven
plate-layers and three signalmen occupying the cottages. There
was a beer-house and a butcher's shop!

Firbank

Firbank, 'the wooded bank', is situated between Dillicar and
Killington. On the east side it is bounded by the River Lune and
on the west by the M6, which divided Firbank from Lambrigg.
Now, I have written about Firbank fairly extensively in my
previous book about the Howgills, so suffice it to say here, that it
is from Firbank churchyard that one of the finest views of the
Howgills is seen. Much in the same way as I crossed over the
Lune to include Firbank in my Howgills book, I intend to cross
over the other way, that is eastwards, to include Middleton and
Barbon, which might otherwise be forgotten altogether! These
two townships were included in the Lonsdale Ward and were
chapelries of Kirby Lonsdale. Today, they are part of the Kirkby
Lonsdale Team Ministry.

Middleton and Barbon provide fine walking country, with
rounded fells similar to the Howgills, and, indeed, they are part
of the same range of hills. At Middleton, many small streams, of
which Lune Gill is the only one of any width, flow westwards
towards the Lune. However, none of these is as significant as
Barbon Beck, a little further south, which may be why there is a
distinct village at Barbon, while with Middleton it is difficult to
know where it begins and ends.

Middleton is 'the middle farm', and the old hall there is said to
be 'the best example of domestic architecture of the fifteenth
century in Westmorland'. Here. the Middleton family lived from
the reign of Edward III until 1644, and the house is well worth
seeing, for it has several original windows and part of the
curtain wall still standing. It is thought that there was once a
pele tower, but nothing of it remains and most likely part of the
present house was built on the site of it.

Another fine house, Beckside Hall, situated next to a farm
called Hollins, the 'holly', was the birthplace of Sir John Otway,
who later lived at Ingmire Hall, nearer Sedbergh. Otway was a
Catholic and, as a Justice of the Peace, evaded the recusancy

laws, it seems, and he is known to have been particularly lenient towards the Quakers in their early days.

The Church of the Holy Ghost, which stands on the west side of the Sedbergh to Kirkby Lonsdale road, was designed by C. J. Ferguson in the Perpendicular style, in 1878. It stands on the site of an earlier chapel built in 1634, and is a humble building compared with the more impressive church, St Bartholomew's, which Paley and Austin were responsible for, in 1893, at Barbon. This has a fine tower with a small staircase turret, and has a general feeling of opulence inside. Barbon was particularly fortunate in its church, and, of course, it was a question of money. Lord Shuttleworth, who owned Barbon Manor, contributed liberally, as did Lord Bective, and there was a considerable legacy from a Mrs Eastham.

Barbon appears as 'Berbrun' in Domesday Book, and it is listed among Tostig's estates. The name seems to mean the 'beaver stream', and it is interesting that there were those industrious animals in this country, as there were in Scandinavia. It was, of course, the Norse who provided the name!

Barbon is a pretty little village centred round the church and the Barbon Inn, a very good place to stop! However, time is short, and I have to travel through Casterton towards Kirkby Lonsdale, and the places west of the town, pausing only to mention the murals by two faded Pre-Raphaelites, James Clarke and Henry Holiday, in the Church of the Holy Trinity, at Casterton. The church was built by Carus-Wilson as a chapel for the school when it moved from Cowan Bridge, so the date must be 1833.

Lupton

Anyone who knows the Kirkby Lonsdale to Kendal road, the A65, will be familiar with Lupton, a village set in a dip where the road curves round. It is just a group of houses, some looking fairly old, with one inn, The Plough, and very little else, yet the place has a long history and, like Barbon, is mentioned in Domesday Book. 'Lupetun' was one of the manors held by Torfin, so, it seems, Torfin and Tostig had this area 'sewn up' between them. Lupton is 'Luppa's farmstead', and is probably named after an early settler, much in the way we have seen before at other places.

The village contains several interesting farmhouses. These include Fowlstone Farm, which stands on the north side of the main road and was built during the seventeenth century. It has the initials of Edward and Anne Burrows and the date, 1655, displayed above the two-storeyed porch. Then, there are two eighteenth-century houses, Thompson Fold and Greenlane End, each worth notice. Greenlane End is one of the houses featured in J. H. Palmer's *Historic Farmhouses in and around Westmorland.*

There were three hamlets within the township of Lupton: Lupton Row, Lupton Smithy and Cow Brow, which, apart from the last mentioned, are no longer distinguished on any map, and even Cow Brow seems to be crammed in as an afterthought. However, this was the hamlet that developed, and was situated about a mile north-west of the small stream, Lupton Beck, on which there was once a mill in operation. The beck rises in Manzergh, flowing from a tarn called Wyndhamere Tarn. We seem to have heard of something quite like it before! To begin with, the beck comes due south, but turns westwards past Spital and Badger Green, meandering north-westwards, and passing beneath the old canal it continues on its course, joining Peasy Beck some three-quarters of a mile before it meets the River Bela.

The church at Lupton, All Saints', is a small neo-Norman building situated north-east of the village, about a mile or so up a narrow lane that leads eventually to Lupton Hall. The church was built in 1867, and inside there is a small wooden font with a conical cover, which is supposed to be the one made for Kirkby Lonsdale during the reign of James II.

Hutton Roof

I am tempted to say that the most interesting thing about Hutton Roof is its name, but that would be unfair, since the village is situated in a most spectacular spot dominated on the western side by Newbiggin Crags and Hutton Roof Crags. But what of the name? We have seen that 'Hutton' has nothing to do with huts, but with hills, and there is no doubt about those here. The 'Roof' is really very simple once one accepts that it is someone's name; the earliest records give the name as 'Rophe' or 'Roffe' in the twelfth century, and in 1256, it was 'Ruffe'. The first 'Roof' appears in 1376, fairly late on the scene, so it would seem to be the farmstead near the end of a hill belonging to him, though we know absolutely nothing about him!

When Ivo de Tailbois granted Kirkby Lonsdale to the monks of St Mary's, York, the land included a portion of the Manor of Hutton Roof; but in 1351, a John de Hutton Roof held the manor from William de Courcy, and later it was granted to Hugh de Moresby by Joan de Coupland in return for homage and knight service of 8s. a year.

Ecclesiastically Hutton Roof was always a chapelry of Kirkby Lonsdale, and there would have been a chapel there in pre-Reformation times, though the present church was built in 1881 to replace the earlier chapel erected in 1757. The present building was another of Austin and Paley's churches, Perpendicular, and, as Nikolaus Pevsner puts it, 'a good, honest job'. There is inside the church on the chancel wall a memorial to Rev. Theodore Bayley Hardy who was Vicar of Hutton Roof for a short while before and during the early years of the First World War. Hardy was killed in action only three weeks before the Armistice was signed, but his bravery while attached to the 8th Battalion of the Somerset Light Infantry earned him the DSO and MC, and when George V visited the battlefield, Hardy was awarded the Victoria Cross and appointed an Honorary Chaplain to the King. There is also a bronze memorial tablet to this brave man, which asks: 'What is courage but the inspiration of the Spirit?', in Carlisle Cathedral.

There was a village school in Hutton Roof, founded by Thomas Chamney in 1773, which for many years flourished in the building erected in 1852, but it was forced to close down through lack of pupils in the 1960s. About a mile south-east of the village is an area known as Hutton Roof Park which during the reign of Edward VI was owned by Judge Carus, though later, it seems to have belonged to the 'vain' Colonel Charteris, whom Alexander Pope satirized in 'Epistle No. IV' to Lord Burlington:

> 'Given to the fool, the mad, the vain, the evil,
> To Ward, to Waters, Charteris, and the Devil.'

Also included in Hutton Roof is the small hamlet, Newbiggin, which is situated near Lupton Beck, and is closer to Lupton than its parent village.

Burton-in-Kendal

Burton-in-Kendal, to give it its full name, was at one time the chief corn market in Westmorland, and until the Kendal and Lancaster Canal was opened in 1819 the Tuesday market there must have been a lively gathering. Corn was brought into the town by the farmers from North Lancashire and auctioned off to the dealers from Kendal and the other neighbouring towns of Kirkby Lonsdale and Sedbergh. Burton was ideally situated for the purpose on the Lancaster to Kendal highroad, and the charter to hold the market had been granted in the second year of Charles II's reign together with two annual fairs, one to be held on St George's Day and the other on Whit Monday. By 1829 the market was described by one eye-witness as more for pleasure than traffic, though 'a few cattle are brought for sale, and a number of farm servants stand to get the straws taken out of their mouths, or in other words to get hired'.

Burton is a good example of how the coming of the railway could reduce, as well as increase, a place's importance. Who would have thought that Oxenholme could assume a greater importance than Burton in the days of Burton's prosperity? Yet, one only has to look about the little street and see the architecture of some of the houses to realize that the place has an affluent past.

Burton is listed in Domesday Book as 'Bortun' and as one of Torfin's manors. The name is derived from *Burh*, meaning a fortification, and *tun*, a farmstead. There are, of course, dozens of Burtons in the country, and several in Westmorland, so that they were usually distinguished by an affix of some kind, as in this case. This linking with Kendal meant that it was within the Barony of Kendal, and not that it was anywhere near the Kent Valley!

Richard I granted Gilbert Fitz-Reinfred two carucates of land in Burton. A carucate was ploughland, and strictly speaking the amount of land one plough and eight oxen could till in a year. Fitz-Reinfred and the Kendal Barons seem to have let Burton to a family that adopted the name of the place. A Roger de Burton represented the county in Parliament, in 1297; but the last member of the family, Anthony de Burton died in 1320, leaving no heir, so that the estate passed to his sister, who was married to Sir Thomas de Betham. The Bethams held Burton until the

close of the fourteenth century; then it appears in a list of estates
granted to Sir James Harrington for his part in the capture of
Henry VI, after the Battle of Hexham. Edward IV granted the
lands 'for services in taking prisoner, and holding as such in
diligence and valour, his enemy, Henry, called King Henry VI of
England'. However, after the Battle of Bosworth, the lands were
all confiscated and reverted to the Crown.

Ecclesiastically, Burton was included in the grant to St
Mary's Abbey, York, by Ivo de Tailbois. The grant had not
originally included the tithes, though these were later added in
1359, so that the priest in charge was, by 1460, reduced to living
on £20 a year 'arising from a house, a yard, and a close called
Kirk Butts, with all small tithes, oblations and mortuaries'.
The poor man had to repair the chancel of the church and
provide candles for the Masses, besides paying the sum of
£1 3s. 4d. to the abbey. I cannot help thinking of Chaucer's Poor
Parson of a Town!

St James's, Burton-in-Kendal, is one of the more interesting
churches in the region and like that of Kirkby Lonsdale has
Norman work incorporated in the restored building, particularly the lower part of the tower and the north-west corner of the
nave, but like all the local churches it was very much rebuilt in
the nineteenth century; this one was 'restored' twice, first in
1844 and again in 1872 when Mrs Hornby of Dalton Hall
contributed three-quarters of the £2,000 needed. The Jacobean
pulpit, dated 1607, is worth noticing and carved fragments of a
late tenth-century cross-shaft which depicts the Harrowing of
Hell.

There are several fine-looking houses in Burton, especially
Burton House built in the late eighteenth century, while there
are Georgian houses on either side of the Market Square. The
market cross seems to date from the days of Burton's prosperity;
it stands some twenty feet high and is a column of local limestone standing on three octagonal tiers of stone steps.

The old county boundary of Westmorland in the south has
become the county boundary of Cumbria. From Kirkby Lonsdale it dips south round Hutton Roof Crags to take in Burton and
then moves shakily westwards, leaving Priest Hutton, Yealand
Redmayne and Silverdale south of the border. It appears from
earlier records that Dalton, a small township originally south-

east of Burton, was at one time in Lancashire, though it seems it was always in Burton Parish, as were at one time Preston Patrick and Holme, while Holmscales, a hamlet in Old Hutton township was also part of Burton ecclesiastically. It was almost certainly all to do with cash, and made Burton a much more attractive proposition for any incumbent.

The area of Burton is dominated by Farleton Knott, or Fell; this is often referred to as the 'Gibraltar of Westmorland' and is really part of a series of fells; Holmepark, Clawthorpe and, a little to the south, Hutton Roof Crags. Here, there is a considerable limestone outcrop, and the hills are interesting walking. Hardly interesting enough, however, to have detoured two walkers who, in the summer of 1818, entered the little market town of Burton. The purpose of these two was to tour the Lakes and the Wordsworth country. Burton was very much busier than usual, as one of the walkers described in a letter to a friend:

> On our arrival quite ready for dinner we turned into the first inn, the Green Dragon, and put up our petition with the usual phrase of 'What could we have?' A voice replied in an instant, and in the gruffest tone. 'Nothing, you can have nothing here!' It was the Green Dragon himself in the shape of a tall, corpulent figure, with the largest face that ever a man was blessed with – a face like a target: and one that a starving traveller might be tempted to shoot at. This unfeeling lump went on to tell us his house was full of soldiers, and that he could neither give us food, nor a room to sit in.
>
> Turning from him into the King's Arms, the landlady there uttered her spleen in a milder strain. She said: 'Ah! gentlemen, the soldiers are upon us! The Lowthers had brought 'em here to be in readiness.'

We know why the soldiers were there! The two friends were unable to find accommodation that night in Burton, so they walked on as far as Endmoor, where they were lucky to obtain a room. One of the friends was called Charles Brown. 'What was the other's name?' someone might ask. His name was Keats. John Keats.

Index